MARRIAGE
DIVORCE
AND REMARRIAGE
in the Bible

Other Titles by Jay Adams

The Christian Counselor's Casebook

The Christian Counselor's Manual

Competent to Counsel

Essays on Biblical Preaching

Essays on Counseling

Handbook of Church Discipline

How to Help People Change

Insight and Creativity in Christian Counseling

The Language of Counseling and the Christian
    Counselor's Wordbook

Lectures on Counseling

Preaching With Purpose

Shepherding God's Flock

Solving Marriage Problems

A Theology of Christian Counseling

Update on Christian Counseling

MARRIAGE
DIVORCE
AND REMARRIAGE
in the Bible

Jay E. Adams

ZondervanPublishingHouse
Academic and Professional Books
Grand Rapids, Michigan

A Division of HarperCollins*Publishers*

Requests for information should be addressed to:
Zondervan Publishing House
Grand Rapids, Michigan 49530

All New Testament quotations are from *The Christian Counselor's New Testament.*

Library of Congress Cataloging in Publication Data

Adams, Jay Edward.
    Marriage, divorce, and remarriage in the Bible.

    (The Jay Adams library)
    Originally published: Phillipsburg, N.J.:
Presbyterian and Reformed Pub. Co., © 1980.
       1. Marriage—Biblical teaching. 2. Divorce—
Biblical teaching.   3. Remarriage—Biblical teachings.
I. Title.   II. Series: Adams, Jay Edward. Jay Adams
library.
BS680.M35A22 1986   234'.165   86-4125
ISBN 0-310-51111-9

Printed in the United States of America

   93   94   95   96 / CH / 16   15   14   13

To Dave and Bill,
whose marriages have been a model for many.

Contents

I work with pastors regularly and have done so for 14 years. I know most of the problems they face. And I know that large on their agenda of areas for study (in which thorny problems grow thickly) is the whole territory of divorce and remarriage. Pastors, as a whole, simply do not know how to handle the knotty questions they are being called upon weekly to face. I am not referring to liberal ministers but to conservatives—Bible-believing, Bible-preaching men!

These pastors want to follow the Scriptures wherever they may lead, but they do not yet see that way clearly. The problem is not, as Dwight Small concludes (after hyper-dispensationalizing half the New Testament[1]), that the Bible has nothing definitive to say on the subject; what is left of *his* Bible may not—but mine does. God surely hasn't left us on our own as Small suggests. No! There is more than enough pertinent revelation concerning the issues involved. Our problem is of a different sort.

We have neglected the whole area for so long, uncritically accepting local or denominational traditions, most of which side-step many of the most crucial problems, that we are at sea. Seminaries often have relegated such "practical matters" to a secondary status, giving to them but a nod in their curricula—if anything—while majoring on many areas that a minister rarely (if ever) encounters in the day-by-day work of the pastorate. So, students go out into churches blissfully unaware of the tangles into which families can twist a marriage, and ill-prepared to do anything constructive.

Those who have attempted to study the territory scripturally have discovered the commentators differ radically, often by-pass crucial issues, and (in general) don't help very much. They also quickly get a taste of the breadth and depth of the subject and become aware of the many complex and knotty exegetical problems that exist. Often, they conclude (reluctantly): "I just don't have the time (or ability) to peel all the layers of this onion; my overloaded schedule simply won't permit me to do it."

So they let it go. But, then, what does one do when he is faced with one of the many sorts of divorce and/or remarriage cases that are, with greater rapidity than ever before, becoming an ordinary part of a pastor's counseling fare? You know, of course. Far too often he finds himself uneasily falling back on the traditions of his congregation (pressures from the board and from members to do so can be great too) even when he suspects (or knows!) that

---

1. In his book, *The Right to Remarry.*

these traditional positions are questionable or ill-founded.

But there is more behind this weak and unsatisfactory response of the conservative church. Until quite recently, the whole area was carefully avoided. This never should have been so; but there were forces at work (see Chapter I) that made it possible (even though it was wrong to do so) for churches to ignore such problems. It was relatively easy for a pastor in past days to say, ''Sorry, I don't marry any divorced persons,'' and for congregations to state in their by-laws that ''No divorced person may teach, sing in the choir or hold office.'' That is how it was. And, in some congregations, perhaps in a considerable number of them, that is still how it is today. But where those positions still prevail, there is a difference—they are held more and more with an uneasy conscience.

Today, divorce is commonplace; it is not just a disease contracted by Hollywood movie stars. It even provides the background for a number of family shows on TV. The stigma of divorce has been all but removed from vast segments of society. New converts, coming into evangelical churches in unprecedented numbers, are as likely to have been divorced (or divorced-and-remarried) as not. They want to know about their status in Christ's church. And (as they should) they are demanding answers based on something better than tradition—they want to know what God's Word has to say.

In response to these new pressures, a spate of books and pamphlets has been forthcoming. But writers have been widely divided about the interpretation of the key passages. Views range from complete permissiveness to tight prohibitions of divorce or remarriage under any circumstances. The great, earth-breaking work of John Murray, *Divorce,* although hesitant and incomplete at so many vital points, still stands as the best of the bunch. But its style is crabbed, its presentation is tedious, its conclusions are often tentative (and sometimes wrong) and its scope is limited. Guy Duty's book, *Divorce and Remarriage,* is useful, but thin, and poorly written. All in all, the Christian church still awaits a comprehensive, lucid, accurate study presented in a readable and practical style that, nevertheless, expounds and does justice to the biblical data.

Whether God, in His providence, will be pleased to use the present volume (at least in part) to fill this gap and meet present needs, only time will tell. In it, I have tried to do what I believe needed to be done, to produce what pastors and laymen everywhere are looking for. It is my prayer that in it they will find what they seek.

Jay Adams
The Millhouse
Juliette, GA, 1980

Introduction

This is not a book on marriage, primarily, though I shall find it necessary to say much about marriage (for more, see my book, *Christian Living in the Home*). There is no way to talk about divorce and remarriage without first discussing marriage.[1] I do not mean that we must discuss marriage exhaustively, but there is a need to consider basic principles. Apart from such a backdrop, the biblical view of divorce and remarriage is difficult to see.

The subjects treated in this book involve questions of great concern to the church. While not every problem will be ironed out in these pages I hope you will agree that quite a few are. Because the issues of divorce and remarriage have been avoided in the recent past, there is very little substantive material available. Commentators briefly discuss them in passing, as they touch upon the pertinent passages. Now and then a sermon here or there deals with some of the easier questions. But fundamentally, the church leadership has floundered and its members are floundering with them.

Twenty-eight years ago, when I officially began my ministry as the pastor of a church in western Pennyslvania, Christians barely talked about marriage and rarely (if ever) had anything to say about divorce and remarriage. It was not that these matters were taboo; it just seemed as if they were unnecessary. Apart from John Murray's book, virtually no one was writing about the questions. Today, of course, the shelves of Christian bookstores are loaded down with books on marriage and divorce (most of which, after flipping the pages, you obviously don't want to read). But back in those pristine days that's the way we were. Why?

We didn't see the need to discuss the family for a number of reasons. For one thing, we were engaged in a life-and-death struggle with liberalism, and we were then losing most of the battles. Christian institutions by the scores had fallen into liberal hands; conservatives had been thrown out of their churches while denominations, one after another, passed into the control of unbelieving leaders. The airwaves (religious TV was only beginning) belonged to liberals. Evolutionists were on top. Conservatives sat in their store-front churches, licking their wounds. There were battles on every hand, but few resources or personnel to which to turn. Actually, in compari-

---

1. In my opinion, this is one reason why so many books on divorce have missed the mark.

son with today's glut of materials, there were very few Christian books printed. The great publishing houses were run and staffed by liberals. Conservative publishers were small and few in number, and the conservative market was minute. Bible-believing Christians were a tiny minority.

Conservatives were hanging on by their toenails. And, in those days, many of them were dispensationalists of the sort who were saying, "It will all be over very soon. This is the eleventh hour. If we can just hold on for another year or two, the Lord will come." That meant little long-range planning, little or no aggressive, forward-looking activities, and minimal concern about families.

Coupled with such attitudes was the fact that there wasn't a great deal of time, energy or resources to produce much. What there was went into defense. Some things had to go by the board. Unfortunately the choice was to major on matters other than those about which this book is concerned.

While this explanation doesn't excuse the church, it does go far toward explaining why a whole generation (mine) grew up with little or no instruction about Christian living (in general) and marriage and the family (in particular). We were left to stumble into all the wrong paths in order to learn (the hard way) what we are now able to pass on to the next generation.

The young minister starting out today lives in an entirely different era. The situation has changed radically. The true church is now on top: it is the liberals who have fallen on bad times. Conservatives now have the major resources and are moving ahead. Their seminaries are chock-full of students, and books on almost every phase of life abound. (Indeed, the problem today is to wade through the plethora of publications to discover which are worthwhile.)

And yet, even with this change, there have been relatively few books (virtually no good ones other than those mentioned in the Preface) on divorce and remarriage. There are anecdotal works, telling about the struggles and heartaches of broken marriages, sermons denouncing divorce, but still little that exegetically or theologically considers these matters. Pastors, as a result, are still at a loss. Their boards are confused. Seminaries largely skirt the subject, and the Christian public is utterly perplexed. Even many issues about marriage itself are still unclear.

Now add to that confusion all the eclectic notions imported from pagan psychological or psychotherapeutic sources and sprinkle in some views from popular, well-meaning (but misguided) speakers and you have all the ingredients needed for a rather bitter brew. There are more books that psychologize the Scriptures when discussing divorce than there are that do serious exegesis in an attempt to understand and explicate them. Obviously, therefore, the need for such materials is great.

But that isn't all. At one time the church thought (wrongly) that it could depend upon society in general to support and instruct its young people about marriage.[2] Educators, politicians, popular leaders, and just about everyone else (including the police departments) took an outward, avowed stand for marriage and against divorce. Marriage and family took a revered seat right next to motherhood, the American flag and apple pie. Thus, an entire generation (or two) grew up knowing that it was in favor of marriage, but not knowing why. We were biblically illiterate about family, marriage, divorce and remarriage.

We are aware of the many differences today—people no longer think of the American flag, motherhood and apple pie as givens. Young people have been burning the flag, ERA adherents and lesbians have been denouncing motherhood, and I fully expect the FDA or the Surgeon General to ban apple pie as "dangerous to your health" in the not-too-distant future. Times have changed. The family has not been immune; along with other axiomatic values, its worth has come into question. Indeed, the family is under strong attack; no wonder divorces abound!

Open marriages of a dozen different varieties are advocated in the schools; TV shows either make divorce and remarriage commonplace and acceptable or glorify them; and young people are being told that marriage is a human invention which we no longer need now that we have "come of age." It has outlived its usefulness and is (at best) the harmless, but unnecessary, vestigial remains of a past era. We have (supposedly) grown beyond the need for marriage as a control over human life. If it is more convenient not to marry in this day when we are no longer naive about contraception, then so be it. After all, marriage has its drawbacks, doesn't it? And if man invented it as an expediency, now that we have the pill and legalized abortion-on-demand, man can do away with marriage as no longer expedient.

Under this sort of attack by liberal theologians, politicians, teachers, medical practitioners and others, Christian youth have become confused. They have grown up with no solid, positive, biblical instruction about marriage from either their parents or the church, and they are now succumbing to bombardment by these negative ideas toward marriage and the family.

This new situation *demands* a new response from the church and the Christian home. We must learn to discuss the basics of marriage and divorce. We can no longer get along by depending on societal institutions to

---

2. This is one reason why we are now in trouble.

do this for us. (In reality, we never could. They always supported marriage for unbiblical reasons and thereby sowed the seeds of its destruction.) If we don't, we can be sure that the world will teach its ideologies. And now that the world has come out of hiding, it is openly expressing the views of the "new morality" that were there all the time—under the table. But it is unthinkable for Christians to stand by idly while our youth are being corrupted.

In the former era, when engaged in pitched battle with liberalism, when resources were so limited, and when society outwardly supported something similar to Christian ideals of marriage and divorce, how easy it must have been to ignore the whole question. Moreover, since there was so little divorce in general (and especially in the church) divorce represented a temptation into which the church was not likely to stumble. The war-weary believer could readily ask (with some justification): "Why beat a sleeping dog? Who's fighting the family anyway? Why bother to spend much time on that subject?" But, though it was not entirely wrong to speak like that then, who can fail to see that it is wrong today? The war is being waged on a different front in our time—the battle lines are being drawn in the home.

In one way, then, we are in a better situation than ever before. This more open, less subtle attack on the family has *forced* the church to go back to the Bible and renew the study of marriage and divorce that for so long was neglected. That is, from the point of view of her responsibility, it is a good thing (though the reasons for the pressure that she feels are very sad).

Unless we come forth *now* with the goods—we can wait no longer—all Christian values will be levelled and, with their counterparts in the unsaved world, the next generation of Christians will grow up following their feelings in these matters rather than following their biblical responsibilities.

Now consider one more factor. In those days, back as far as I can remember, most churches simply didn't deal with questions of divorce and remarriage because (as I intimated) it wasn't a live issue. Divorce was virtually an unheard of problem among Christians as recently as 25 years ago. Thus, the church was able to close her eyes to the subject. That was convenient, because divorce is messy and the biblical passages are not easily understood. Then, too, converts were few, so there weren't as many persons already divorced coming into the church as there are today. Moreover, society (as I have noted) frowned on divorce and even passed laws that made it difficult so that there were far fewer divorces outside of the church as well. The conservative churches, backed by this ethos in the general society, had very few cases with which to contend. Largely, they pursued a hands-off policy. There were notable exceptions, of course. But, as a whole, the conservative churches drifted on in blissful ignorance, too far "above" such sordid, mundane matters to take the time and trouble to study and resolve the many perplexing (not to say vexing) questions connected to this whole area. But there came a rude awakening when the tables quickly turned, the new morality came top side up, and the church was suddenly caught unawares and tongue-tied.

It was easy for the church to assume a holier-than-thou attitude while there were so few cases to face (these could be avoided). In those few instances, there were lives wrecked along the way, of course. But weren't these people suspect anyway?

Some survived such treatment, on their own. Others wandered off (to who knows where?). Many were kept out of offices, from teaching, even from singing in choirs because they were "divorced persons"—and thus, became second-class citizens in God's kingdom.[3]

And most pastors never, never remarried divorced persons (no matter what the circumstances); that was understood across the board. Pastors successfully defended their positions with policy statements: "I'm sorry; I just don't marry divorced persons." No questions were asked about the past—a divorce had occurred; that was enough! The attitude has not died out entirely. Today, in certain quarters it persists and indeed, is being strengthened by teaching currently being spread throughout the USA.

So, that's something of the background for our discussion. That is how we got to where we are. Well, if that is so, where are we?

We are living in a culture in transition. We live in a time when all the old values have been challenged (both within and without the church). They have been pulled up by the roots, thrown up into the air, and are now beginning to come down like tossed salad.

(1) Christians are confused. They aren't sure what to believe.
(2) They don't know how much is tradition and how much is biblical.
(3) They want to reject the traditions of men in favor of a more biblical stance,
(4) But they don't know where to find the help that they need.

Personally, I like this sort of day. It opens opportunities to think biblically in a fresh way, unhampered by prejudicial views that really have no warrant for acceptance by people who wish to be biblical. It is a great time in which

---

3. Often, it mattered little whether they were "innocent" or "guilty," whether the divorce was biblically legitimate or not; to be a "divorced person" was enough to disqualify one (despite repentance, gifts, etc.).

to minister the Word. Yet, it has its own temptations. Radicalism—of the sort that throws out everything, bad and good—thrives in such a period. Fear of radicalism, on the other hand, can stifle good change and true advance in thought. But we must not allow extremes to impede progress in understanding and applying the Scriptures. The great advantage of a time like this is that conservative Christians are willing to pay serious attention to new views, provided they are truly biblical. To explore the Scriptures and to arrive at more concrete, more definite biblical positions is my concern in this book. I want to be as biblical as possible. The reader must decide whether or not I have succeeded.

There are no other options. The church is suffering. Divorced persons are flooding into our congregations. Remarriages are taking place everywhere. Is this right? Is it wrong? On what bases are divorced persons being dealt with? These and a host of similar questions simply cannot be ignored any longer. Because I think that I have some answers (though not all of them) I would be remiss in not trying to clear up as many problems as I can. You hold in your hands the results of my efforts.

I said that I like the fact that the church can no longer avoid this area. That is true; the frequency of inquiries and the enormity of the present problem has led to innumerable requests for such a book.

I recognize that this book comes too late to help many. But, perhaps, we can catch up a bit and then prevent more *faux pas*.

I recognize also that there are many people who want to sweep the whole problem under the rug. That fact must not stop us. Nor should we slow down because of the peril involved. I speak of *peril* advisedly. There are some— perhaps more than I know—for whom this is the most explosive of all possible issues. Gossip, schism, even adultery itself (as they see it), all seem to be forgivable; but divorce? Never! It is a highly emotional issue for them, and they have a hard time even reconsidering afresh what the Bible has to say about divorce and remarriage because of their strong feelings. That is why there is some peril to writing about divorce and remarriage. I trust that if you are one whose feelings about this subject are intense, you will do at least three things:

(1) Don't write me off. Hear me out—consider seriously what I have to say, even if you must reject it.
(2) Recognize that my desire is to honor Christ by being as scriptural as I can be.
(3) Try to lay your prejudice aside and to curb your emotions as you read.

For the sake of Christ's church I must write, whatever the risk.

Of course, that's only one part of the story. There are many—an ever increasing number—who are no longer content to bury their heads in the sand. They want to know what the Bible teaches about these matters and how they can implement that teaching in counseling others and in their own lives. It is especially for them that this book has been written.

PART I

MARRIAGE

CHAPTER 1

Some Basic Considerations about Marriage

We must begin here. Do not skip over part one. There is no way in which divorce—the dissolution of marriage—or remarriage after divorce can be considered until certain very essential biblical facts about marriage itself have been established. Too often, those who discuss problems connected with divorce misunderstand (and misinterpret) the biblical data precisely because they have not taken the time to develop a biblical view of marriage. Care in doing so is vital: the two hang (or fall) together.

I shall not consider marriage in depth, but only those aspects of the subject that are absolutely essential for reaching a proper scriptural position on divorce and remarriage. In this book, then, the accent will fall upon these two questions. The study of marriage is the road to the study of divorce.

Since divorce is the dissolution of marriage ("putting asunder what God has joined together"), it is necessary for us to discover and understand plainly what it is that divorce dissolves and how.

Some, for instance, speak as though a divorce doesn't necessarily dissolve a marriage. They talk about some divorced persons as "still married in God's sight." Is this a valid concept? The language isn't biblical; is the idea? If so, how is it that Christ warns about "putting asunder" what cannot be put asunder?

Or, does a divorce really bring an end to a marriage, not only legally but also before the Lord? Then, Christ's warning may be considered straightforwardly as a warning against doing something that we should not do.

This issue is not academic; the resolution of the problem has a number of very important practical implications for life. And they cannot be avoided by any thinking Christian. But to resolve the problem by answering the question, one must first know what it is that establishes a marriage. How is a marriage made? What is its status before God?

What Is Marriage?

Contrary to much contemporary thought and teaching, marriage is not a human expedience. It wasn't devised by man, somewhere along the way in the course of human history, as a convenient way of sorting out responsibili-

3

ties for children, etc. Instead, God tells us that He Himself established, instituted and ordained marriage at the *beginning* of human history (Gen. 2, 3).

God designed marriage as the foundational element of all human society. Before there was (formally speaking) a church, a school, a business instituted, God formally instituted marriage, declaring, "A man shall leave his father and mother and shall cleave to his wife, and the two shall become one flesh."[1] It is important to teach this fact to young people.

If marriage were of human origin, then human beings would have a right to set it aside. But since God instituted marriage, only He has the right to do so. He has told us that marriage will not be dispensed with until the life to come.[2] Nor can marriage be regulated according to human whims. Marriage as an institution (which includes individual marriages, of course) is subject to the rules and regulations set down by God. If He had said nothing more about marriage after establishing it, we might have proceeded to draw up such rules on our own. But He did not leave us in the dark; God has revealed His will about marriage in the pages of the Bible. Individuals may marry, be divorced and be remarried only if, when and how He says they may without sinning. We must, therefore, study and abide by the biblical principles for marriage. Neither a private individual nor the state has any competence to decide who may be married (or divorced) and on what basis. The state has been given the task of keeping orderly records, etc., but it has no right (or competence) to determine the rules for marriage and for divorce; that prerogative is God's. He has revealed His will on these matters in the Scriptures which are expounded and applied by the church.

Secondly, marriage is a foundational institution. We have seen that it was the first to be instituted formally as a sphere of human society. Society itself in all its forms depends on marriage. The attack on marriage, experienced today, is actually an attack on society itself (and on God, who built society on marriage). Marriage is also the foundation upon which the church as God's special society rests. This covenantal community is weakened as the "house" or "household" is weakened. (The "house" in Scripture is the smallest unit of society. It is a group of persons, living under the same roof, under one human head, and is a separate decision-making unit.) This "house" (equivalent to our "family," but a richer concept) is a unit with

---

1. Gen. 2:24. Informally, of course, the church, work, education, etc. were all present from the outset. But only marriage was established *as an institution* from the garden.

2. Mark 12:25; Luke 17:26, 27.

which God deals *as a unit*.[3] Therefore, the attack on marriage (around which a "house" is formed) is an attack on the basic sub-unit of the church.

For all these reasons, an attack on the family is no light matter. Rather, at once, it constitutes an attack upon God's order in the world and in His church.

Thirdly, marriage is not what Roman Catholic theology and many Protestants (wrongly) have thought—an institution designed to propagate the human race. While God has ordained that procreation must be carried on as one duty in marriage ("Be fruitful, and multiply"), and only within marriage, procreation is not the fundamental feature of marriage.

To maintain, as some do, that marriage *per se* is biologically necessary for procreation is nonsense and confuses everything. In particular, such thinking confounds and confuses marriage with mating. The human race (like gerbils, white mice, goats, etc.) could propagate itself quite adequately apart from marriage by mating. Ghettos in which there are very weak marriages, if any, grow enormously from mating disconnected from marriage.

No. Marriage is something more than mating. While marriage includes mating as one of its duties, the two must not be identified. To reduce marriage to legalized, responsible mating, therefore, is an error with serious implications. The propagation of the race is a sub-purpose of marriage, not the major purpose. Human beings would, if anything, be even more prolific than they are if there were no marriage institution.

Fourthly, it is important to understand that marriage must not be equated with sexual relations. A sexual union is not (as some who study the Bible carelessly think) to be equated with the marriage union.[4] Marriage is a union that implies sexual union as a central obligation and pleasure (I Cor. 7:3-5), it is true, but sexual union does not necessarily imply marriage. Marriage is different from, bigger than, and inclusive of sexual union (just as it is inclusive of the obligation to propagate the race), but the two are not the same.

---

3. Just as God deals with individuals, nations, the church, congregations, He *also* deals with "houses." Cf. Gen. 7:1; 19:12-14; Josh. 2:19; 6:23; Deut. 11:6; Acts 16:31; John 4:53; Acts 10:2; 18:8. According to Josh. 7:14, God divided the nation into tribes, clans, houses (families) and individuals. The word "house" is used of physical dwellings, the temple and tabernacle, the church (I Tim. 3:5), a family line (tribe; Matt. 10:6; Luke 2:4) and individual families; Mark 6:4; Acts 7:10; 16:31. A "house" included all who were under the roof (and thereby under the authority of the head) of a house. This included slaves, relatives, etc. In David's case (Ps. 101:2) it was his palace, and all who dwelt in it. But it might be as small as one married couple dwelling by themselves.

4. Cf. Exod. 22:16, 17 (Berkeley). Clearly, if they had to be married later, they were not married already; and if the father refused, they never would be.

5

If marriage and sexual union were one and the same, the Bible could not speak about illicit sexual intercourse; instead (in referring to fornication) it would talk about informal marriage. Adultery would no longer be adultery, but informal bigamy (or polygamy). But the Bible does speak of sexual sin outside of marriage and doesn't give the slightest credence to the notion that adultery is bigamy. Throughout, the Scriptures refer to marriage, in itself, as something other than and distinct from sexual union (licit or illicit). The words *marriage* and *fornication* (*porneia*, which means any, and all, sexual sin[5]) cannot be equated.

Though it may be easy in the abstract to accept this fact that sexual relations do not constitute marriage, when we come to the matter of divorce, we so often find people humming a different tune. Some erroneously say that adultery itself dissolves marriage because a new marriage is made.[6] But that is not true either, biblically speaking. Some say, "Well, it's dissolved in God's sight." But that sort of language (and the thinking behind it) has no biblical support. The notion that the marriage begins on the honeymoon when sexual relations first occur, and not when the vows are taken is totally foreign to the Scriptures. On the former basis, the pastor would be lying when he says, "I now pronounce you man and wife." Nonetheless, a marriage is consummated when a man and woman exchange vows before God and each other, and they enter into a covenantal relationship. The minister officiating at the wedding is telling the truth.

Marriage *authorizes* sexual relations. The honeymoon union is proper and holy (Heb. 13:4) only *because* the young couple is already married. And adultery, later on, while exerting tremendous strains on the marriage, does *not* dissolve it. Sexual relations *per se* do not *make* a marrriage and do not *break* a marriage.

Divorce, following adultery as a consequence, therefore, is not merely an outward recognition and formalizing of an inner reality, but a new and further step beyond (and not necessitated by) the adultery. It is not proper to *remarry* a couple if and when forgiveness for adultery is sought and obtained and the two decide to continue to live together. They are still married; forgiveness alone[7] is necessary.

This point—that sexual relations do not constitute a marriage—is abso-

5. This matter will be discussed in depth at a later point.

6. If adultery dissolved a marriage God could not say to the Israelite adulterers, ". . . she *is* your companion and your wife *by covenant*" (Mal. 2:14b). She would no longer be either, and He would not have referred to the covenant as He did.

7. Of course, in the single word forgiveness I am including repentance and seeking both God's and one's spouse's forgiveness.

lutely essential to any proper understanding of marriage, divorce and remarriage. Marriage is bigger than and distinct from (though inclusive of the obligation of) sexual union. It is neither constituted nor dissolved by sexual relations.

If marriage is not to be equated with sexual union or with the propagation of the race, we must look for the essence of marriage elsewhere.[8] What is marriage, we ask again? The answer to that all-important question will be found and discussed in the next chapter.

---

8. For more on this, see my book, *More than Redemption* (Phillipsburg, N. J.: Presbyterian and Reformed Publishing Co., 1979), pp. 129ff.

CHAPTER 2

What Marriage Is All About

We have taken a preliminary look at the origin and the importance of marriage, and at some false understandings of marriage that had to be cleared away. We have seen how essential marriage is to society, in general, and to the church in particular. But we now must ask the question, once again, What is marriage?

Our answer to that question will lay a foundation for our discussion of divorce and remarriage after divorce.

It is time for Christians to make crystal clear what God has said about this matter. There has been too much guessing, philosophizing and psychologizing instead. There is no need, and no excuse, for any of this: God has spoken clearly. His Word is so explicit that there is no room for speculation and doubt.

God's own answer to the question is found in Genesis 2:18:

> It is not good for the man to be alone. I will make him a helper who approximates [or corresponds to] him.

In other words, the reason for marriage is *to solve the problem of loneliness*.

Marriage was established because Adam was alone, and that was not good. *Companionship,* therefore, is the essence of marriage. We shall see that the Bible explicitly speaks of marriage as *The Covenant of Companionship*.

Marriage and the Single Life

God's fundamental evaluation of the single life is that it is "not good." That is what He says, and in that word lies the reason for the general rule that "a man shall leave his father and his mother and shall cleave to his wife and the two shall become one flesh" (Gen. 2:24).

Sin, however, has so distorted society and so twisted human beings in their relationships to God and to one another that some do live lonely, single lives despite this rule and its provision. But also, because of the crisis nature of life from time to time brought about by sin, and because of the urgent demands upon God's church at all times to spread the good news and to build up weak Christians in their faith, God has called some to be exceptions to His

8

own rule and provided for their need of companionship by gifting them especially to lead the single life (cf. Matt. 19:11, 12; I Cor. 7:7).

According to Matthew 19:11, 12 and I Corinthians 7:7, there are people whom, we might say, God has singled out for Himself to lead a life of celibacy for the sake of His kingdom. Jesus speaks more fully about this matter in Matthew 19:11, 12 than at any other place. After the discussion of divorce (vv. 3-9) in which Jesus said that fornication (sexual sin) is the only permissible ground for divorce among believers, the disciples commented, "It would be better not to get married then."[1] They thought, presumably, if marriage is that permanent, it would be better not to run the risk of marrying the wrong person. But in reply Jesus said, "Not everyone has the capacity for that, but only those to whom it has been given" (v.11). It is clear from this response (as well as from I Cor. 7:7) that there are exceptions to the rule given in Genesis 2:18, 24. And since the gift of celibacy is a gift from God, it is also clear that He has made the exception to His own rule. This gift is never explained clearly in detail, but doubtless, in it is the "capacity" to find companionship of a different (it could never be the same) sort outside of marriage in the special kingdom works to which some are called. This seems implied in verse 12:

> There are eunuchs who were born that way, there are eunuchs who were made eunuchs by men, and there are eunuchs who make themselves eunuchs [i.e., refrain from marriage] for the sake of the empire from the heavens (v. 12).

The latter part of this verse indicates that these single persons have been gifted with the capacity to live satisfying (not lonely) lives by (in one way or another) becoming deeply involved in the work of the Lord in ways that married persons cannot (cf. I Cor. 7:32-34).

Note the conclusion to verse 12: "Whoever has the capacity must exercise it."[2] He leaves no options open; God gives no useless gifts. Those who have the gift for marriage (I Cor. 7:7) must prepare for marriage and seek it. Those who have the gift to pursue the single life, likewise, must prepare for it and pursue it. The former group sins by purposely avoiding marriage; the latter,

---

1. Verse 10. Incidentally, according to I Cor. 9:5, they all did marry.
2. Many Christian singles are sad and lonely because they have not tested their gifts to determine whether or not they have been granted the special gift of *single service* for Christ's empire. One can determine this by applying the tests in Matt. 19 and I Cor. 7:8, 9. He must test to see (1) whether lifelong sexual containment is a possibility, and (2) whether he finds satisfaction and companionship in the work of God's kingdom. (When one does nothing special in the kingdom, and pursues his own "career," he or she cannot know, or expect to find, the answer to loneliness. The gift must be exercised for God.)

9

by contracting it. Each person must search for and then exercise his gifts and the capacities that come along with them. There must be no complaints about God's wisdom in dispensing His gifts—He does all things well.

Before asking other questions, or complaining that "God must have passed me by," etc., one ought to ask the basic question: "Am I one of those whom God has singled out?" When one can honestly answer that question definitively, he will find no need to ask most of the rest (and he surely will not have cause to complain).

The single life is not according to the rule set forth in Genesis 2:18; it is exceptional. But precisely because it constitutes an exception (that God Himself, by gifting, has made), it ought to be specially recognized in the church for what it is. Christian singles ought not to be looked down upon by marrieds or neglected (as so often they are). Rather, they ought to be honored for the special efforts they make in pursuit of the special kingdom tasks to which God has called them. That doesn't mean pinning medals on them, but it does mean conferring honor on those to whom honor is due. After all, Paul was one of those special people; we don't look down on him, do we?[3]

Someone may wonder how I Corinthians 7:8, 26 can be squared with Genesis 2:18. In the latter verse Moses writes that "It is *not good* to be alone"; in the former, Paul says it is "good" to be single as he was. Do the two contradict?

No. The general rule of Genesis 2:18 applies to most people, and (in general) has always been true. The exception given in I Corinthians 7 (in addition to the one we have studied in Matthew 19) applies to extraordinary circumstances ("Because of the impending crisis"—I Cor. 7:26[4]). The general rule is true for most, under most circumstances. But it may be set aside in times of persecution. In a time of great persecution, similar to the Neronian blood-bath that Paul (as a prophet) was anticipating, this passage comes into play. Both are "good" for different persons, in different situations. (Of course, neither exception would have been necessary if Adam had not sinned. The general rule was stated prior to that sin.)

But even in times of persecution, persons who have difficulty "containing" do not sin if they follow the general rule and marry (or give their children in marriage—cf. I Cor. 7:27-31). The persons advised to pursue the

---

3. It is possible (but not probable) that Paul had once been married. But surely, at the time of writing I Cor. he wasn't. He could have been a widower or his wife could have left him (possibly even divorced him) because of his conversion to Christianity.

4. See also v. 29.

single life in Matthew 19 are to do so, not because of an impending crisis, but because there are special tasks that God has for them to do. Those who are advised to pursue the single life (if possible) in I Corinthians 7 are (in contrast) those who, under other conditions, would be urged to marry. Indeed, even married persons must forego some of the otherwise normal privileges and activities of married life (I Cor. 7:29).

The Covenant of Companionship

Now we must consider in detail what we have already seen to be the very essence of marriage: *companionship*. God made most of us so that we would be lonely without an intimate companion with whom to live. God provided Eve not only (or even primarily) as Adam's helper (though help is also one dimension of companionship), but as his companion. He too, as all other husbands since (we shall see), is to provide companionship for her.

In the Bible marriage is described in terms of companionship. In Proverbs 2:17, for example, we are told that "the strange woman . . . forsakes the *companion* of her youth and forgets the covenant of her God.''[5] The word translated *companion* in this verse has in it the idea of "one that is *tamed*" (it is used in speaking of tame animals), or "one that has a *close, intimate* relationship to another." It is hard to establish a close relationship with a wild animal, but one can be on close terms with a domesticated (or tame) animal. The core meaning has to do with a close, intimate relationship. And that is exactly what marriage companionship is: the close, intimate relationship of a husband and wife to one another. "Wild" attitudes or actions on the part of either destroy companionship; "tame" (warm, willing to be close) actions and attitudes foster it. Companionship, then (at least in part), involves closeness.

The concept of marriage as companionship also appears in Malachi 2:14, where a different, but very complementary, term is used:

> The Lord has been witness between you and the wife of your youth to whom you have been faithless, although she is your *companion* and your wife by covenant.

Now, the word here translated "companion" has as its kernel idea that of *union* or *association*. A companion, therefore, is one with whom one enters into *a close union* (or relationship). In putting the two terms together, we come to a full sense of the idea of companionship. A companion is one with

---

5: Strange (or "foreign") woman = an adulteress. She is called a foreigner because neither harlots nor adulteresses had any place in Israel.

whom you are intimately united in thoughts, goals, plans, efforts (and, in the case of marriage, in bodies).

The two passages, together,[6] make it clear that for both the husband and for the wife, companionship is the ideal. In Proverbs, the husband is called the companion (showing that he too provides companionship for his wife); in Malachi, it is the wife who is so designated. For *both*, then, entrance into marriage should mean the desire to meet each other's need for companionship. Love, in marriage, focuses upon giving one's spouse the companionship he/she needs to eliminate loneliness.

These facts have not been faithfully taught in the church, and need to be asserted repeatedly wherever one can get a hearing—in sermons, in young marrieds' groups, in older couples' meetings, to teens, to children. If there is such a fundamental ignorance of God's teachings about marriage, no wonder, then, that what He says about divorce and remarriage is misunderstood.

Engagement for Marriage

We must now turn to the important matter of engagement in the Bible. Today, in our quite different culture, most Christians have little or no understanding of what a biblical engagement was like, and what it involved. Modern practices must not be read back into the biblical accounts.

Engagement, for us, is often a trial period. Many look on it as *officially* going steady with some intent to marry. There is nothing really binding about it. In the Bible, on the other hand, an engagement was absolutely binding. In effect, it was the first step of marriage. In the engagement the marriage covenant was made,[7] and an engagement could be broken only by death or by divorce (Deut. 22:23; Matt. 1:16-24).

An engaged person who willingly entered into illicit sexual relations with another did not incur a fine, but (as in adulterous relations after marriage) was put to death (cf. Deut. 22:23 N.B., the engaged girl is called the "wife" of the man to whom she is engaged). Indeed, contrary to the views of some, there is every biblical reason for referring to illicit sexual relations during engagement as nothing less than adultery.

In contrast to an engaged person, the single individual who entered into illicit sexual relations underwent a lesser penalty (Deut. 22:28, 29).[8] The

6. The words for companionship are used interchangeably as their use in parallel construction in Micah 7:5 indicates.

7. Cf. Douglas, *The New Bible Commentary*, (Grand Rapids: Eerdmans, 1962), p. 788.

8. Whether the marriage would occur, in such cases, was at the father's discretion according to the fuller passage in Exod. 22: 16, 17. Surely, the girl's wishes were to be considered.

point, therefore, to keep in mind is that engaged parties were given the same penalty as married persons (cf. Deut. 22:22). No distinction whatever was made.

The same usage that we noted in Deuteronomy 22:23, where we see that engaged parties are referred to as *husband* and *wife,* occurs consistently elsewhere in the Scriptures, confirming the high view of engagement that persisted (cf. II Sam. 3:14; Matt. 1:19). In the last cited passage,[9] Joseph is plainly called Mary's "husband," even though it is explicitly said that they had not come together in sexual union (Matt. 1:25).

A few additional comments on the events recorded in Matthew 1 might be helpful. Matthew tells us that Joseph had decided to *divorce* Mary secretly (v. 19). Probably by this time divorce had come to replace stoning. Possibly, under Roman law, punishment by stoning for this offense was not allowed. Some, however, conjecture that stoning was rarely, if ever, used (perhaps that was involved in what Jesus called the "hardness of men's hearts"[10] that he said influenced Moses). The facts regarding this substitution (or change) are not clear. But because in that very verse Joseph is called a "just man" (plainly a commendation of his contemplated action), it seems evident that (at that time, anyway) God did not look with disfavor either on the substitution of divorce for stoning or, N.B., on the idea of divorce itself for illicit sexual relations. This interesting fact has implications that bear upon later considerations.

But, for now, notice that the marriage which began with engagement (and required a divorce to break) did not begin with a sexual union (Matt. 1:25) and had to be ended by divorce.

All these facts make it as clear as can be that marriage is fundamentally a contractual arrangement (called in Mal. 2:14 a marriage "by covenant") and not a sexual union. Marriage is a formal (covenantal) arrangement between two persons to become each other's loving companions for life. In marriage, they contract to keep each other from ever being lonely so long as they shall live. Our modern wedding ceremonies should stress this point more fully than they do.

We have no engagement or wedding ceremonies of any detail in the Bible. The closest thing to a ritual or ceremony of engagement (or practice that possibly preceded the engagement ceremonies) is found in Ruth and Ezek-

---

9. Probably, also in vv. 20, 24 the translation should read "take Mary, your wife" and "took Mary, his wife" rather than "Mary *as* his wife."

10. What men might call softness God could call hardness if it was a hardness of heart toward God's laws and ordinances. But this explanation does not seem very likely.

iel. The practice is not altogether clear to us, but, in some way or other, involved spreading one's garment over the woman to be engaged (cf. Ruth 3:9, 10). In Ezekiel 16:8 (Berkeley) we read,

> When I passed by you again, I observed that you were of age for courting; so I spread out the skirts of My robe over you and covered your nakedness. I plighted My troth to you and entered into covenant with you, says the Lord God, and you became Mine.

Here, God becomes engaged to Israel by spreading His garment over her, thus taking her under His protective care.[11] The plighting of the troth (or lit., swearing, taking of vows) to her may refer to the engagement (or possibly to the wedding later on[12]). In Hosea 2:19, 20, God speaks of becoming engaged[13] to Israel "forever" and "in faithfulness" (cf. Berkeley). The lasting nature of the engagement stands out in the passage. When he goes on to say, "And you shall know the Lord," he is echoing a covenantal phrase.

We have no other marriage ceremonies in the Bible. The closest thing to a wedding ceremony appears in the apochryphal book of Tobit. But this is not necessarily typical, since it seems to be a condensed, sped-up version of the normal thing. There are exceptions, doubtless.

With the marriage of most virgins, the engagement period lasted from 9 to 12 months. For a widow, there was but a three month period of engagement.[14] But since Tobias (Tobit's son) was going to get his wife from a great distance, everything is compressed. For what it is worth, this is what we read:

> Then he called his daugher Sarah, and taking her by the hand he gave her to Tobias to be his wife, saying, Here she is; take her according to the law of Moses, and take her with you to your father. And he blessed them. Next, he called his wife Edna, and took a scroll and wrote out the contract; and they set their seals to it. Then they began to eat (Tobit 7:13ff. RSV).

And did they eat—for 14 days! (18:19).

Note the elements in this marriage ceremony (which we have no reason to believe to be atypical):

1. The father "gives away" his daughter, formally taking her by hand to

---

11. The word for *garment* in Ruth and *skirt* in Ezekiel also means "wing." The idea of the protective wing is common (Ps. 36:7; Exod. 25:20). In engagement, the girl came under the protective care and concern of the boy.

12. It would seem that the vows were made at the engagement.

13. Again, "swearing" is involved.

14. Cf. *Everyday Life in Bible Times* (National Geographic Society, n.p., 1967), pp. 305, 306. See also *Talmud, Kethuboth* 57.

his son-in-law.

2. He verbally pronounces the fact: "Here she is, take her. . . ."
3. He blesses them both.
4. He and his wife write out a formal marriage contract.
5. They validate it with their seals.
6. There is a public wedding feast.
7. They "escorted Tobias in to her" (8:1).

The ordinary ceremonies probably were very similar. One thing seems clear: the marriage ceremony included formal, contractual elements that were placed on record. And there was a public ceremony. Though the process was simple, the contractual side is prominent.[15]

All along I have referred to marriage as a covenantal arrangement. I should like to say a word or two more on that point before concluding this chapter. Marriage, I have called (with good biblical reason) a *Covenant of Companionship*.

Turning once more to Proverbs 2:17 and Malachi 2:14 (not to mention Ezek. 16:8, 9 to which I referred earlier), note that forsaking the companion of one's youth is paralleled with forgetting the covenant of God (Prov. 2:17). In Hebrew poetry, such synonymous parallelism is used to equate two things while expressing different aspects of a subject. Forsaking a companion is the same as forgetting the marriage covenant.

In Malachi 2:14, a similar concept emerges. There, God denounces husbands who are faithless to their companions. These companions are further described as those who are wives by covenant (NASB). So, in both passages where companionship is prominently mentioned, so is the covenantal aspect of marriage. That means that (as I have pointed out) marriage is a *Covenant of Companionship*.

In this covenant, two people covenant not only to bear and raise children, to satisfy each other's sexual needs, etc.; these goals are too narrow (though they are a part of the larger goal). The two agree (by vows; lit. by "swearing"—cf. Hos. 2:19, 20; Ezek. 16:8) to live together (Matt. 1:18, NTEE) as companions in order to take away each other's loneliness. (This includes both factors mentioned above, but also many others.)

That covenant, we have seen, is made at the time of engagement by contract (not by sexual union), but the two begin to fulfill all the terms of the covenant only after the wedding ceremony and celebration when they

---

15. Greek marriage contracts from the NT period are even more formal. Cf. Hunt and Edgar *Select Papyri* (Cambridge, Mass., Harvard U. Press, 1970), vol. I, pp. 2-23. These contracts, interestingly, spell out the particulars involving possible divorce.

actually begin to live together.

Other Factors

I have been speaking of other factors included in companionship. What are some of these?

Genesis 2:18, 24 tell us much. The word *helpmeet,* which has come into the English language, is a hybrid-word. When a husband says, "Meet my helpmeet," he says two things. In 1611, when the King James Version of the Bible was translated, verse 18 read, "I will make him a help meet for him." The words *help* and *meet* were written separately as two distinct terms. Later, in popular parlance, there was an eliding of the two into one word. In 1611, *help* meant exactly what our present-day word *helper* means; *meet* meant *appropriate to, corresponding to* or *approximating at every point.* So, God says, I will make him a helper who is appropriate to him. Meet, appropriate to, suitable for, etc., are all translations of a Hebrew word that has in it the notion of *over against* or *approximating.* We might appropriately speak of Eve as Adam's *other half* (not better half), which in the covenantal union of marriage makes a complete whole. This *other* half approximates Adam at every point.

As his counterpart, the woman completes or fills out the man's life, making him a larger person than he could have been alone, bringing into his frame of reference a new feminine dimension from which to view life that he could have known in no other way. Then, too, he also brings to his wife a masculine perspective that enlarges her life, making her a fuller, more complete person than she could have been apart from him. This marriage union by covenant solves the problem of loneliness not merely by filling a gap, but by overfilling it. More than mere presence is involved. The loneliness of mere masculinity or femininity is likewise met.

Helping, mentioned in the verse, is another aspect of companionship. The two are united as companions in effort (cf. the woman's orientation toward her husband's work in Prov. 31). Some of the richest joys of companionship stem from working side by side with one's spouse. Whatever one does, he needs an interested helper by his side. Ultimately, they work together for the Lord (this is the fundamental unifying factor in marriage—they marry "in the Lord") whatever the specific tasks at hand may be at any given point. There is someone with whom he (she) can talk things over, someone to counsel, someone to care; to share joys, perplexities, ideas, fears, sorrows and disappointments: a helper. A marriage companion is someone with whom one can let down his/her hair!

This fact comes out even more fully in Genesis 2:24, 25 where marriage is described as a *cleaving* (clinging or adhering) in which a man and his wife become "one flesh," and in which they were able to be naked in each other's presence without shame.

The phrase "one flesh" needs explanation since it is frequently misunderstood. It does not refer (primarily) to sexual union (though that is included in it). The words closely parallel our English compound word, *everybody*. When we say every*body* we do not think of *bodies* only. Rather, we mean every*one*, every *person*. Hebrew usage was similar: "all flesh," for instance, means everyone (everybody, every person: cf. Gen. 6:17; 7:22; 8:21). When God speaks of destroying *all flesh*, He doesn't mean flesh in distinction from bones. What He means is "I shall destroy every *person*." When Joel (also quoted in Acts 2 by Peter at Pentecost) wrote of God pouring out His Spirit on "all flesh," again, what he had in mind was *every sort of person* (Jew, gentile, old, young, male, female). So, here, in Genesis 2:24, to "become one flesh" means *to become one person*.

The marriage union is the closest, most intimate of all human relationships. Two persons may begin to think, act, feel as one. They are able to so interpenetrate one another's lives that they become one, a functioning unit. Paul, quoting this verse in Ephesians 5:28-31, says that the relationship is to be so intimate that whatever a man does (good or evil) for his wife, he also does for himself since the two have become one flesh (person).

Even in I Corinthians 6, where, at first, one might think of the use of the verse as confirming the sexual aspect of marriage, a more careful reading shows otherwise. Paul distinguishes three sorts of unions:
1. one *body* (v. 16)—sexual relation with a harlot=a close union
2. one flesh (v. 16)—the marriage union=a closer union
3. one spirit (v. 17)—union with Christ=the closest union

It is not possible here to develop this important passage further.

God's revealed goal for a husband and wife is to become one *in all areas of their relationship*—intellectually, emotionally, physically. The Covenant of Companionship was designed to fill this need.

Today, people everywhere are trying to establish close, open relationships in other ways. The Covenant of Companionship was designed to fill this need, and only it can do so. Weekend marathons, group therapy sessions, etc. will not do the job. God ordained marriage for this purpose; human substitutes will fail. Because marriages are failing, people try (vainly) to find satisfaction elsewhere.

In verse 25, Moses refers to nakedness without shame. This, too, has been interpreted sexually (wrongly). The shame has to do with sin; since Adam and Eve were sinless, they were shameless. They were able to be perfectly open, transparent and vulnerable to one another.[16] They had nothing to hide. That still is the ideal for marriage—openness without fear or shame. Two persons with nothing to hide could be utterly frank; there was no need to have anything to come between them—not even clothes. They were entirely open to one another. Openness groups will not satisfy; marriage alone provides the right setting for openness. When the marriage rests on Christian truth and is energized by Christian living, that is possible. Truth unifies, love binds and hope orients. These elements allow for openness without shame.

Such a view of marriage shows plainly that marriage is far more than legalized mating (Mating=one body; marriage=one flesh). Companionship makes the difference. In marriage counseling, therefore, the Christian counselor is not uncertain about his objectives. He knows that to glorify God, he must develop and foster deeper companionship between husbands and wives. In this way, marriage once again may begin to approximate the ideals that God set forth in Genesis 2.

NOTE

In biblical times, a marriage did not require approval and licensure by the state, as it does today in our culture. In biblical times, contracts were drawn up and executed by the parties in concern with witnesses and could be used, if necessary, as legal documents. We must distinguish so called "trial marriages" and "marriages of convenience" from true, biblical marriage. Two college students who "shack up" for the semester, or until graduation, are not married; they are committing fornication. There has been no contract—verbal or otherwise (no swearing of vows or promises were made)—so there is no marriage. On the other hand, *irregular* marriages may and do occur. If a man and woman, cast up on a desert island, make vows to one another, they are married—even without the state's approval. However, as law-abiding Christians, upon rescue, they will immediately regularize their relationship by asking the ship's captain to perform the wedding ceremony required by the state. The question to pursue in all cases involving irregular "marriages" is whether some agreement (verbal or otherwise) was made by the parties. A wife (according to Mal. 2:14) is "a wife *by covenant*." This factor also applies to all so-called "common law marriages."

16. Cf. Heb. 4:13—"Before Him no creature can hide, but all are naked and vulnerable to the eyes of Him to Whom we must give an account."

Marriage is not only the principal building block of society in general, and of the church in particular, but it also occupies a key place in human life.

Genesis 2:24 has other important facets. Everyone who has done any counseling at all soon becomes aware of the fact that there are more family and marriage problems than all the rest put together. This demonstrates its central focus in human affairs. He also discovers, by looking more closely, that great difficulties arise when a man or woman puts activities, things or other persons in the places that God has accorded to his spouse and his family. We are told that the man must "leave" his father and mother and "cleave" to his wife.

God did not put a parent and child into the garden. Adam and Eve were man and wife. That shows that the primary human relationship (and family relationship) is husband and wife. That is why a man must *leave* father and mother and *cleave* to his wife. The first relationship is temporary and must be broken; the second is permanent, and must not be broken. Divorce always is the result of sin, therefore.

There is no covenantal promise made by parents and children to meet each other's needs for companionship as there is in marriage. Whenever either parent or child tries to find it there, rather than in the marriage itself, difficulties arise.

The man, in particular, is said to "leave," not in order to exclude the wife (as though she need not leave), but because it is he who must become the *head* of a new decision-making unit, that (we have seen) is called a "house"[1] (or "household"). As such, he may seek and receive advice, but not commands from his father and mother. There is always tragedy in the wind when a husband puts his parents over himself (thus denying his headship) or in the place of his wife (thus denying her first place in his life). The latter problem is especially acute when he allows himself to be pulled in two directions by the two women (mother and wife).[2] I am tempted to work

---

1. See, especially, the comments on this term in a footnote in chap. 1.
2. For more on these problems, see my book, *Christian Living in the Home*, pp. 51-56.

19

out the detailed implications of failure to "leave" in every sense of the term (physical, mental, etc.) but must not here. In the pages just cited in the preceding footnote, I have done so already.

When wives vainly attempt to fight loneliness by substituting children (especially a son) for husbands, or when husbands try to do so by burying themselves in business (or busyness), they err greatly. Under God, a husband and a wife must put one another first, before all others, and all activities. Only in that way will children be free to leave home without heartache when the time comes. And, the marriage will grow.

The relationship between parent and child is established through birth (or adoption); the relationship between husband and wife, by covenant promises. Blood may be thicker than water, but it should not be thicker than promise. This contrast between the temporary parent-child relationship and the permanent husband-wife union once again forcefully points up the uniqueness of marriage in God's plan for human beings.

Since this description of marriage focuses on covenantal companionship, it is obvious that one must cultivate companionship.[3] A marriage lacking companionship is headed toward misery or divorce. All that jeopardizes companionship must be avoided; whatever promotes it must be cultivated.[4]

---

3. A book on this subject, showing how to do so, is Wayne Mack's, *How to Develop Deep Unity in the Marriage Relationship* (Phillipsburg, N. J.: Presbyterian and Reformed Publishing Co., 1978).

4. Communication, for instance, is one essential to companionship. See *Christian Living in the Home*, pp. 25-41 for a full discussion of this all-important issue.

PART II DIVORCE

CHAPTER 4

A Biblical Attitude Toward Divorce

Contrary to some opinions, the concept of divorce is biblical. The Bible recognizes and regulates divorce. Certain provisions are made for it. This must be affirmed clearly and without hesitation. Because divorce is a biblical concept, used and referred to frequently in the pages of the Bible, Christians must do all they can to understand it and to teach what God, in His Word, says about it. Moreover, the church is required to apply to actual cases the Scriptural principles regarding divorce.

There are some, nevertheless, who so conceive of divorce that, if you followed their thinking you would have to conclude that the Bible makes no provisions for divorce, but (rather) only condemns and denounces it. They would lead one to believe that Scripture says nothing—absolutely nothing—positive about divorce. Yet, as we have seen, Joseph (a just man) was not condemned for determining to divorce Mary. So, there must be more to the divorce question than some think.

To begin with, let us be clear about the fact that neither is the Bible silent on the subject of divorce, nor does it always, under all circumstances, for everyone, condemn divorce. That much must be established from the outset.

While God emphatically says, "I hate divorce" (Mal. 2:16), that statement must not be taken absolutely to mean that there is *nothing* about divorce that could be anything but detestable, because He, Himself, also tells us

> . . . for all the adulteries which faithless Israel had done, I sent her away and gave her a divorce bill (Jer. 3:8, Berkeley).

If God Himself became involved in divorce proceedings with Israel, it is surely wrong to condemn any and all divorce out of hand. Obviously, from this passage (and the passage from Matt. 1) it is certain that sometimes, in some ways, divorce, for some persons, under some circumstances is altogether proper and not the object of God's hatred.

It is altogether true that God hates divorce. But He neither hates all divorces in the same way nor hates every aspect of divorce. He hates what occasions *every* divorce—even the one that *He* gave to sinful Israel. He hates the results that often flow to children and to injured parties of a divorce (yet even that did not stop Him from willing divorce in Ezra 10:44, 11). And he hates divorces wrongly obtained on grounds that He has not sanctioned. But that leaves some things about divorce that He does not hate. He certainly does not condemn or hate divorce proceedings *per se*—i.e., as a process. Nor does He hate divorce when it is obtained according to the principles and regulations laid down in the Scriptures and which He followed in His dealings with unfaithful Israel.

Already, I think you must see, the matter cannot be treated so simplistically. To say, therefore, "I'll have nothing to do with divorced persons" is to speak irresponsibly and, to boot, places one in the unenviable position of having nothing to do with God! (He is a divorced Person!)

Your attitude about divorce is important—because your attitude will show in your relationship toward, and your dealings with, divorced persons. If you discover that you have a bad attitude, as you very well may if you have grown up in a totally anti-divorce climate, you will find it getting in the way of your counseling of those contemplating divorce as well as in your work with divorcees and in your approach to those seeking to remarry.

It is important, therefore, to develop a balanced, biblical attitude toward divorce—on the one hand, hating all those things that God hates about divorce, while recognizing that in this sinful world there are those situations in which (as God Himself demonstrated) it may be necessary to obtain a divorce.[1] Your position, obviously, will affect your attitude. So it is quite important to understand and adopt a truly biblical position.

There are many wrong attitudes in the conservative churches about divorce and divorcees. From the way that some treat divorced persons, you would think that they had committed the unpardonable sin. Let us make it clear, then, that those who wrongly (sinfully) obtain a divorce must not be excused for what they have done; it *is* sin. But precisely because it is sin, it is forgivable. The sin of divorcing one's mate on unbiblical grounds is bad, not only because of the misery it occasions, but especially because it is an offense against a holy God. But it is not so indelibly imprinted in the life of the sinner that it cannot be washed away by Christ's blood.

Indeed, it is noteworthy to discover that in those lists of heinous sins (I Cor. 6:9-10; Rev. 22:15; Gal. 5:19-21, etc.) selfishness, envy and other

---

1. Cf. also Ezra 10:2, 3, 11, 19. Here it is plain that a "covenant with God" was made to divorce foreign wives. And it is said explicitly that this was done to "honor" God "by doing what He wills" (v. 11, Berkeley). It was done in faith, in a period of repentance (cf. v. 19), N.B., *in covenant* with God. One hundred and thirteen divorces took place, out of repentance, to honor God. Surely, not all divorce is wrong, in itself, even though all divorces—including these—are occasioned by sin.

somewhat unexpected items (like slander) take their place side by side with drunkenness, idolatry, murder and homosexuality, but not once is there mentioned the sin of unlawful divorce.

My noting this fact does not mean for a moment that I want to tolerate improper divorce, or any divorce sinfully acquired; divorce wrongfully entered into is sin and must be labelled and condemned as such. No, my purpose in pointing out the absence of any reference to sinful divorce is merely to observe that the apostles must have had a much different concept of divorce than those present-day church leaders who always include it in their lists of most hated sins—often near or at the top. I do not want to minimize the sin of improper divorce in all of this, I remind you. It is heinous; such divorce may not be tolerated. But what I am urging is a proper (biblical) attitude on the part of God's church. To fail in this is serious; many lives (including the whole church) cannot escape the adverse effects—all will be hurt.

Since divorce is not the unpardonable sin, it can be forgiven. That, of course, does not heal all the heartbreaks of children and in-laws, not to speak of the parties involved in the divorce. I don't mean to say that it does. Divorce, even when proper, always is occasioned by someone's sin. At its best, then, divorce always brings misery and hurt. That is why God hates it. But, even one who sinfully obtains a divorce can be forgiven, cleansed and restored to Christ's church, just like those repentant drunkards and homosexuals who are mentioned in I Corinthians 6:9-11. They, too, can be washed and sanctified by the same Spirit. We must not call unclean those whom God has cleansed!

When Jesus spoke about the unpardonable sin, He carefully assured us about the forgivability of other sins—all other sins—when He declared:

. . . all sorts of sin and blasphemies will be forgiven . . . (Matt. 12:31).

All other sins can be forgiven. And since obtaining a divorce for sinful reasons falls into that category, we must conclude that it too is a forgivable sin. The only sin that can never be forgiven is the sin of attributing the work of the *Holy* Spirit to an *unclean* spirit. Christ allows no one to call the Holy Spirit unclean! Only those unsaved persons, whose views and values are so turned around as to think that biblical holiness is sinful, could commit such a sin.[2] Divorce can be, has been, is being and will continue to be forgiven by God. His church, therefore, dare do no less.

---

2. For more on the unpardonable sin, see my book, *The Christian Counselor's Manual*, pp. 426-428.

Your attitude must be biblical, no matter what the prevailing climate of opinion of others may be.[3] If your attitude is wrong, you must change it. If others around you have improper attitudes, you must try to influence them to become more biblical. But until you yourself change, you won't be able to help others; the best way to teach others is still by demonstrating it in your own life.

When someone comes up to you and asks, "Did you know that Dave and Mabel are getting a divorce?," how do you respond? Do you gasp for air in shocked disbelief? Or, in deep concern, do you express a truly biblical attitude? Perhaps you could say something like, "I'm sorry to hear that. Do you think we can do something to help them to work out their problems some other way?" Most people don't think that there is much hope when people have gone that far. There is—take it from one who has seen scores of marriages at this point turn around again. In discussing the question, you may even remark that "if we knew the facts, however, divorce, while always undesirable may be the only option open to one of them." Answers like these help others to look at the situation in a realistic, concerned, biblical way that provides a proper response which focuses on data rather than emotions and feelings. Surely, even divorce can be discussed this way.

---

3. Even if you suffer persecution and ostracism. There are some people who become very emotional over the question of divorce who have a very simplistic view and have not even attempted to understand the biblical viewpoint set forth here.

How did divorce begin? No one knows. It's origins lie somewhere back in the dusty past of human history. Unlike marriage, divorce is a human institution. The available (biblical) evidence shows that although divorce is recognized, permitted and regulated in the Bible (as we have already seen), unlike marriage, it was not instituted by God. The Scriptures record no act of God, either directly, or through His prophets and apostles, in which He established, or institutionalized, divorce. God did not originate the concept as a part of His order for society. Divorce, then, is a human innovation.

Jesus' comments on divorce reinforce this conclusion. Instead of speaking of divorce as part of God's order, He specifically recognized it as constituting a change: "from the beginning this was not the way it was" (Matt. 19:8). He further observed that it was only because of the Jews' hard hearts that Moses "allowed" divorce (Matt. 19:8).[1] To allow for (or permit) a practice is not the same as originating, establishing or instituting it. What one "permits" is already in existence as a concept or a practice. The fact that God did not establish divorce (but permits it under certain conditions) is one reason why the church has had a problem in its consideration of the practice.

Divorce first begins to appear as a biblical concept in passages that recognize it as a *fait accompli*[2] over which God (through Moses) exercised a regulating function (cf. Deut. 22:19, 29; 24:1-4). Because Moses regulated, rather than forbade divorce outright, Jesus can say (quite accurately) that Moses "allowed" it. Divorce, then, already was a common practice when Moses wrote the Pentateuch and gave its laws to the people.

If Moses "allowed" divorce by regulating rather than forbidding it, we must never get the idea that God merely winked at divorce. He neither

---

1. The word *epitrepo* means precisely that: *allow* or *permit*.

2. Indeed, divorce first appears in the biblical record as a full-blown practice, indicating that by then it was well known and established. There are a technical vocabulary, legal formulae affixed to it (bill of divorcement) and a step by step process by which it was obtained. Divorce, in the OT, is mentioned this way in Lev. 21:7, 14; 22:13; Num. 30:9; Deut. 22:19, 29; 24:1-4; Isa. 50:1; Jer. 3:1, 8; Ezek. 44:22; Mal. 2:14, 16.

ignores it (hoping that it will go away), nor in toto (as a practice) denounces it, but, rather, takes cognizance of it and does something about it (1) to see to it that divorce is permitted only under certain circumstances, and not under others (cf. Deut. 22:19, 29), (2) that when it is done it is done in an orderly fashion, and (3) that those who obtain a divorce are fully aware of the possible consequences (cf. Deut. 24:1-4). It is certainly correct to say that in the Scriptures God acknowledges the existence of divorce and carefully regulates it.

Our stance, then, must be the same. We must neither wink at divorce, nor simply denounce it (both extremes are unbiblical), but as leaders and officers of Christ's church, we too must seek to regulate it among God's people according to the principle set forth in the Bible.

The Process of Divorce

In biblical times, how did divorce take place? Interestingly, the Scriptures provide more detail about the process of divorce than they do about engagements or wedding ceremonies. Properly handled, a divorce was a formal, legal act whereby the covenant of companionship was repudiated and dissolved. In Deuteronomy 24:1-4, we see that it was a three step procedure. The divorce did not actually take place until all three steps had been pursued:

> When a man has married a wife and comes to dislike her, having found something improper in her, and he writes her a bill of divorce and, putting it in her hand, sends her from his house, and she goes off and becomes the wife of another, and her second husband, likewise comes to her and also gives her a bill of divorce and sends her away, or if the second husband dies, in such case, the man who first divorced her, may not take her again to be his wife, for she has been defiled: such practice is abhorrent to the Lord, and you must not bring such guilt upon the land which the Lord your God is giving you for your heritage (Berkeley).

This passage was not given primarily to set forth this three step process (although it does; we shall examine Deut. 24:1-4 in much more depth concerning its prime intent later on). The divorce was final only when:

1. *There was a written bill of divorce* (Deut. 24:1ff.; Jer. 3:8, etc.). This bill of divorce (lit. of "cutting off") had to be
   a. written
   b. in a form that said it clearly.
Writing the bill made the divorce a legal matter. The bill was probably signed by witnesses, as we shall see. The bill protected the one who received it from false accusations, misunderstandings, etc., and clearly set forth her status as unmarried. To write a bill required time (a person could not, in

anger, divorce another verbally;[3] writing made the act deliberate and premeditated as well as legal).

2. *The bill must be served* (Deut. 24:1). The one who divorced another had to
   a. personally
   b. put the bill into the other party's hand.

Again, time was gained. Others could intervene, etc. But, contrary to Talmudic practice, presumably no third party could serve the bill.

3. *The person divorced must be sent from the home* (Deut. 24:1). The actual rupture of the home must formally occur. The actual conditions in which it was no longer possible to give companionship must come into being. A break in the relationship in which bags were packed and taken by the party leaving must occur. The person divorced must move out of the house.

The Bible gives no sample of a divorce bill (some think Hos. 2:4, "She is not my wife nor am I her husband" was taken from such a bill), but there are divorce bills from later periods that have been uncovered.[4] Here is one:

> On the _____ day of the week _____ in the month _____ in the year _____ from the beginning of the world, according to the common computation in the province of _____ I _____ son of _____ by whatever name I may be known, of the town of _____ with entire consent of mind, and without any constraint, have divorced, dismissed and expelled thee _____ daughter of _____ by whatever name thou art called, of the town of _____ who has been my wife hitherto; But now I have dismissed thee _____ the daughter of _____ by whatever name thou art called, of the town of _____ so as to be free at thy own disposal, to marry whomsoever thou pleasest, without hindrance from anyone from this day for ever. Thou art therefore free for anyone [who would marry thee]. Let this be thy bill of divorce from me, a writing of separation and explusion, according to the law of Moses and Israel.
>
>   _____, son of _____, witness
>   _____, son of _____, witness[5]

---

3. This was a good bit more stringent than the verbal divorce allowed in other cultures where one need only to say "I divorce you" three times for it to take effect.

4. Cf. photographic reproduction in *Encyclopedia Judaica* (New York: Macmillan, 1971), vol. 6, p. 123.

5. W. W. Davies, *International Standard Bible Encyclopaedia* (Grand Rapids: Eerdmans, 1949), vol. II, p. 865. Cf. Guy Duty, *Divorce and Remarriage* (Minneapolis: Bethany Fellowship, 1967), pp. 34, 35 for a similar sample. The phrase *ho thelei* in I Cor. 7:39, probably originated in divorce bill formulae; cf. A. Deissmann, *Light from the Ancient East* (Grand Rapids: Baker, 1978), p. 324.

If this actually approximates the biblical bill of divorce, then the following points may be noted:

1. This bill of divorce was a formal, public document, signed by witnesses, and intended to stand as a legal record for any necessary future use.
2. The stated intention of the divorce bill was not only to effect the permanent separation of the divorce parties, and thereby relieve them from the obligations of the Covenant of Companionship, but also to expressly give the divorcee the freedom to remarry.
3. The bill itself—not just writings about divorce—plainly uses a variety of terms to express the concept of divorce (*divorce, dismiss, expel, separate*) as do Greek divorces in the New Testament and the biblical writings themselves.

Speaking of New Testament divorce, there are also a number of bills extant from the New Testament period that must have been characteristic of those used in the Mediterranean world in which the members of most of the early churches lived. In Volume I, *Select Papyri* (The Loeb Classical Library), there are five marriage contracts and three bills of divorce. The forms, like their Hebrew counterparts, show some variation, but on the major points all are similar. In them, too, the same three facts that we have seen to be true about the Hebrew form also hold true. In these Greek bills of divorce specific mention is made of the divorced party's freedom to marry (". . . and hereafter it shall be lawful both for Zois to marry another man and for Antipater to marry another woman . . . she is free to depart and marry whom she chooses"[6]). Also true is the presence of a variety of Greek terms for divorce. This point will take on added significance as we begin to study the principal New Testament passages in depth at a later point.[7]

God hates divorce.[8] He did not institute it; He only recognizes and regulates it under certain biblically-prescribed circumstances. But—and this is the important concept to gain from reading this chapter—even though God hates divorce, because there is sin behind every divorce as its cause, *not every divorce is sinful.* Some are proper (remember Jer. 3:8; Matt. 1:19). God permitted divorce within stringently defined limits. There are legitimate causes for divorce, even though (perhaps it would be better to say *because*) those causes involved sin. Even though all divorces are the result of sin, not all divorces are sinful.

---

6. Hunt and Edgar, *Select Papyri* (Cambridge, Mass.: Harvard, 1970), vol. I, pp. 23, 24, 27.

7. Let me say only this here, that *chorizo* is used frequently in these bills to mean *separation by divorce.* This point will be of great importance to our study.

8. Remember, not the bill, or the process, but the sin involved in it.

The Christian's stance, then, is that divorce is never desirable, and (among Christians) it is never inevitable. Reconciliation, as we shall see *infra*, is always possible for believers under the care and discipline of the church. While permitted for Christians in cases of sexual sin, divorce is never required. These facts ought to guide us into a basic stance toward divorce, by building a biblical concept into our thinking that will affect our attitudes. Divorce, though a reality that will not go away, is a sad commentary on the hardness of men's hearts, as Christ told us.

A final comment: God permitted and regulated divorce. But He did not *merely* regulate it. The *fact* of regulation indicates His permission (one does not regulate that which He forbids). And the *content* of the regulation indicates (1) that He wished to keep people from doing more damage to one another than they might otherwise, and (2) that He intended to discourage foolish and hasty divorce actions. A study of Deuteronomy 24:1-4, for example, reveals that the process and regulation outlined there both tended to discourage divorce transacted without adequate forethought, and divorce as a handy convenience.

When we study that passage later on, we shall see that it was intended to forbid divorce and then remarriage to the same party if that party had been remarried and later divorced again. This he forbade because it greatly polluted the land. Serial and trial marriages and divorces, with the possibility of return if one later happened to change his/her mind, were not permitted. One had to think twice before committing himself to the almost certain finality that divorce had in that culture under that regulation.

Every legitimate effort, therefore, ought to be made to help persons contemplating divorce to reconsider the alternatives, and to assist divorced persons to become reconciled to one another (whenever possible) before they remarry another and it is too late to do so.[9]

9. That was Paul's emphasis, we shall see, in I Cor. 7:11, where (doubtless) he had the Deut. 24:1-4 regulation in mind.

We have seen that marriage is a Covenant of Companionship. A divorce, then, is the repudiation and breaking of that covenant (or agreement) in which both parties promised to provide companionship (in all its ramifications) for one another. A divorce is, in effect, a declaration that these promises are no longer expected, required or permitted.

By obliterating these obligations, a divorce is intended to free the parties to make the same commitment to someone else. Of course, we have not yet established this biblically, though we have seen that this was the intention in the divorce documents cited. When the divorce (in both its cause and proceedings) was proper (biblically speaking) that is also what it did.

The word for *divorce* in the OT that occurs in the phrase "bill of divorce" (Deut. 24; Isa. 50:1; Jer. 3:8) means "to cut off."[1] The most prominent NT word [2] means "to loose from, to put from, put away, send, release or dismiss." All these ideas are inherent in the word. In Moulton and Milligan, *The Vocabulary of the Greek New Testament*, pp. 66, 67, one can see the import of the word in other contexts. For instance, *apoluo* is used of someone who is *relieved* of his present occupation. Here, the idea is that the association has been broken. In another source, *apoluo* is used to express the idea of *permission to leave* a country, and in still another, it is used of a veteran who is *released* from long service.

However you view it, the concept of divorce has in it the idea of severing of the covenantal relationship that previously existed. Marriage began formally, contractually; when severed not by death, but by divorce, that is

---

1. The bill of divorce=*sepher kerithuth* (bill or certificate of "cutting off"). The other party was indeed *cut off* by the one divorcing her/him. Also, responsibilities to keep the promises of the marriage covenant were cut off (or terminated). Other OT words are used (especially *garash*=to "expel, put away"; cf. Lev. 21:7, 14; 22:13; Num. 30:10; Ezek. 44:22), and *shalach*=to "dismiss, send away, let go, put away;" cf. Deut. 21:14; 22:19, 29; Deut. 24:1, 3, 4; Isa. 50:1; Jer. 3:1; 3:8).

2. *Apoluo*=divorce by putting away. The NT also uses the phrase "a bill of divorce" (from *LXX, biblion apostasiou*). A very important term is *chorizo*=to separate by divorce. The word must be considered later. The last word of importance—*aphiemi*, "leave, send away, divorce"=to leave by divorce.

also done formally, contractually. The notion of the severance (cutting off) and the resultant separation of the parties is prominent, whether that separation is viewed from the perspective of the one who leaves (*aphiemi*), from the perspective of the one who sends the other party away (*apoluo*) or from the perspective of others who see the separation that is the ultimate outcome of the divorce proceedings (*chorizo*).

Separation

A few, initial comments on the word *chorizo*, "to separate" (by divorce) have already been made. One or two other facts ought to be brought to light at this point, and (still later) more must be said.

In the Bible, the modern idea of *separation as something less than divorce* (whether legal or otherwise) was totally unknown as a viable alternative to divorce. Wherever the word separation (*chorizo*) appears in the NT in connection with divorce,[3] therefore, it always refers to *separation by divorce*.

---

3. Cf. Matt. 19:6; I Cor. 7:10, 11, 15. The modern view of separation is an anti-biblical substitution for the biblical requirement of reconciliation or (in some cases) divorce. These two options alone are given by God. Modern separation settles nothing; it amounts to a refusal to face issues and set them to rest. The world may have no way of solving problems—and so opts for an uneasy cease-fire—but the church does, if she will only avail herself of the biblical means. Of all things, separation (in its modern form) tends most to disrupt the peace that God enjoins (I Cor. 7:15c). It keeps all parties involved on the end of the line, playing them like a fish in the water dancing on its tail. It violates the command in I Cor. 7:5, disregards its warning and sets both husband and wife in a place of unnecessary temptation. The problem is that Christians, of all persons, are prone to turn to separation, not only like others who disobey God's command for reconciliation to take place, but especially when divorce is called for (I Cor. 7:15). They think "Well, at least we aren't divorced!" This is because divorce—in *all* instances (even when justified biblically)—has been widely made out to be the great sin of all sins. It is time to say that in certain situations, separation can be worse—especially as a substitute for biblical action.

Can separation provide for a "cooling off period" as some claim? Hardly, since it constitutes disobedience to God's commands (I Cor. 7:5 views it as often leading to a heating up of the furnaces when they ought to be cool; marriage alone cools them—cf.v. 9). Moreover, every counselor knows that the way to put people together is not by taking them apart. Separation heats up desire that it shouldn't, but cools concern that it ought not. The cooling that often occurs is due to a sense of relief from the previous problems, a false sense of peace that is interpreted (wrongly) as a solution to the problem. Nothing actually has been solved. But because of this temporary relief, it is very difficult to effect reconciliation. Often one (or both) of the parties says "I never had it so good" and is loathe to rock the boat. That peace will leave in time, but for some time can be so great a deterrent to reconciliation that it can destroy the prospects altogether. Separation is another means of running from problems instead of solving them God's way.

The first thing a Christian counselor must do, when dealing with separated persons, is to bring them back together again (at this point their great reluctance to return will be seen) so that he can help them to work on their problems in a context (marriage) where solutions can be reached. Two people, under separate roofs, will find it nearly impossible to solve problems that

The word views divorce from the standpoint of the completion of the 3-step process delineated in Deuteronomy 24:1-4—the bill has been written and served, the wife has been sent off, and the two are now *separated* by the process. This is the same standpoint that appears in Matthew 19:6 where Jesus says, ". . . what God has yoked together, a human being must not separate [*chorizo*]." Moulton and Milligan write: "The word has almost become a technical term in connection with divorce."[4] As I observed in a footnote in an earlier chapter, *chorizo* appears regularly in bills of divorce[5] and even in pagan marriage contracts where the possibility of divorce often was taken into consideration.[6]

The word separation (*chorizo*) is used in I Corinthians 7: 10, 11, where the wife is urged not to *separate* from her husband and the husband is encouraged not to leave (*aphiemi*=leave, divorce or send away) his wife (v. 11b). But, N.B., Paul makes it clear that if the wife does indeed disobey this command and separates (*chorizo*), she must remain *unmarried* (*agamos*, v. 11a). Thus, the separation that he has in view in this passage is separation by divorce. We know this because it was a separation that resulted in an *agamos*, or *unmarried*, state. Paul was thinking of the finalized result of the divorce process—separation—because his concern was what might (and should not) occur next (remarriage to another rather than reconciliation). If he had had in mind some form of lesser-than-divorce separation, he could not have written "she must remain unmarried," because she would not yet be *unmarried*. This point will be of significance later on.

Note also that *aphiemi* (divorce, leave), as Paul uses it (v. 11b) in conjunction with the husband, provides the other side of the command. It is set over against "separate" (*chorizo*) as the parallel or equivalent synonym in the command. The wife is commanded not to separate from the husband by divorce, and the husband is commanded not to "divorce, leave (by

---

occur when they are under the same roof. Separation, therefore, only widens gaps and deepens difficulties.

Of course, very brief separations (a couple of hours, an overnight at a friend's house)—where one doesn't pack his/her bags and has no intention of leaving—may at times (when one is violent, confused, etc.) be desirable. But in such a case the brief separation is to *avoid* situations that destroy problem-solving and make communication impossible. The design (in contrast to extended separation, no matter what is said or thought to the contrary) is *to make it possible* to face and solve problems God's way—not to *avoid* them.

4. Op. cit., p. 696. In my opinion, the word "almost" could be eliminated; it *is* a technical term for divorce.

5. *Select Papyri*, vol. I, p. 123—"Zois and Antipater agree that they have *separated* from each other severing the union that they had formed on the basis of an agreement made. . . ."

6. Ibid., pp. 15, 17.

divorcing) or (possibly) send away" his wife (*aphiemi*). Clearly, several words (as was the custom) are used in speaking of divorce.

We have seen, so far, what divorce is and something of how the biblical writers (and persons in the contemporary culture) viewed it. Before going on, it is important to have in mind what we have learned in these first six chapters. Therefore, I urge you—if you have any basic misgivings or uneasiness about what you have read so far—go back, reread, study and rethink what we have covered before proceeding further. In that way, I believe, you will benefit most from the exegetical studies, positions and applications to cases that follow.

CHAPTER 7

The Two Groups in I Corinthians 7

It might seem strange to open our discussion of the biblical passages on divorce with a study of I Corinthians 7. But because so many of the key words and concepts are found there, and because in it there is a comparison and contrast between the two possible divorce situations that the NT considers, and because Paul interprets the words of Jesus and places them in their proper context, I Corinthians 7 is an excellent starting point.

I shall not confine my comments to I Corinthians 7 in this chapter (or in those that follow, in which I take my lead from I Corinthians 7) but rather use Paul's discussion as the base from which to look at other passages as well.

Moreover, since I have already considered I Corinthians 7 from the viewpoint of marriage and the single person, I shall not retrace those lines. My remarks, then, will focus on what Paul says in I Corinthians 7 about divorce and whatever else that may illuminate his words. Paul had the good sense to sort out various items for separate consideration in the book of I Corinthians but he also grouped matters pertaining to the same basic area. Here, marriage and divorce are considered side by side.

Now to the study of important matters. In verse 10 Paul introduces his comments on divorce with these words:

I give this authoritative instruction (not I but the Lord). . .

But in verse 12 he writes:

To the rest I (not the Lord) say. . .

Those two introductory phrases introduce us immediately to two distinct groups of persons: (1) a first group; (2) a second group called "the rest." (I shall consider the words to the second group more fully in the next chapter). These two introductory phrases have (unnecessarily) troubled many Christians. Some think that the first group is divinely commanded, while the second receives only Paul's pious advice. They wonder about the two levels of authority that such a notion introduces into the Scriptures. Is the first comment inspired and the second not? Are both inspired and inerrant but of different weight?

Let us answer all such questions at the outset by observing that they stem from a common misunderstanding of Paul's words. There is no uninspired, errant, nonauthoritative Scripture. That kind of distinction was the furthest thing from Paul's mind.

Well, then, what did he mean by his introductory phrases? Here is what he had in mind:

1. In verses 10, 11, Paul says (in effect), "I am repeating—in a concrete way—the principles about divorce that the Lord [Jesus Christ] set forth in His teaching when He was with the disciples and spoke about divorce among God's people."
2. But in verses 12-16, he says (in effect), "Now I am going to deal with a question that did not arise, and, therefore, that Jesus did not mention when He lived among us. This issue has arisen now that the gospel has gone out among pagans, and I shall address myself to it on my own (in an inspired way, of course, just as I have spoken of many other questions of this sort in this very letter)."

Paul, then, writing as an inerrant apostle, is *adding* to the teaching on divorce that Jesus gave us by dealing with *an additional issue*. That is the point of the disjunction between the two groups addressed.

But—notice well—sometimes when we add, we also subtract. That is to say, by distinguishing between two groups, Paul *limits* the application of Christ's teaching in the gospels to the group addressed in I Corinthians 7: 10, 11. He makes it clear that what Jesus had to say contained not only some general, overarching principles that are widely applicable (like "from the beginning it was not so," and "the two shall become one flesh"), but also some that refer only to persons who fit into the group mentioned in I Corinthians 7:10, 11).

Because of this distinction between two groups, I Corinthians 7 becomes a pivotal passage on divorce and the logical place from which to begin a study of divorce. Not only does Paul place the Lord's teaching in its proper setting (a fully covenantal context in which both marriage partners are Christians), but by doing so, he structures and interprets the Lord's teaching so that we may not go wrong by applying it wrongly or too broadly. Many in their discussion of divorce have almost entirely neglected the important implications of this fact. As a result, their conclusions have been unbiblical, and the consequences in the lives of those instructed by them disastrous.

I shall consider it established, then, that not everything that Jesus said about divorce applies to everyone—or (at the very least) His words do not apply to everyone in the same way. This is not to take anything away from Christ's words; rather, it is to give them their true and full import. But we must not misuse His words by applying them to that about which He never intended to speak. What Paul is saying—and we *must* understand this clearly—is that Jesus never intended to say the last word on divorce. Jesus was speaking within a context that must be recognized for what it was.

Who are the two groups? As a quick glance at I Corinthians 7: 10, 11, 12-16 shows, Jesus was speaking about divorce among believers. In verses 10, 11, Paul addresses the same group, two believers contemplating divorce. But in verses 12-16, Paul goes on to address those Christians contemplating divorce who are married to unbelievers. Jesus, Paul says, had not referred to such a group at all. The question was being addressed for the first time in the NT.

Paul indicates (not only by the directions given to each group, but also by the very structure of setting them apart into two groups) that God's approach to both groups is not the same. Indeed, this is not something unusual. Throughout the Scriptures, situations involving these same groups show that each must be dealt with differently. (Ezra 10 is clear enough evidence of this.[1]) In other areas of life, the relationship of believers to unbelievers also is treated differently than the relationship between two believers. In this very book of I Corinthians, Paul has consistently made that point.

When speaking of going to law, Paul makes it clear that believers may not take other believers into court. Matters can (must) be settled within the church itself. But believers are not prohibited from taking unbelievers to court. In I Corinthians 5, the relationship of Christians to sinning believers and to sinning unbelievers (again) differs widely. Romans 12:18 sums up the general principle for dealing with unbelievers:

If possible, so far as it depends upon you, be at peace with everybody.

It isn't always possible to achieve a peaceful relationship with unbelievers; therefore, the believer is required to do *everything he can* to effect peace, but no more. The principle at work among believers is found in Matthew 18:15ff, where it is assumed that believers have resources from God and His church adequate to resolve all interpersonal difficulties.[2] When an unbeliever fails to respond to the believer's efforts to establish peace, the believer

---

1. In that instance, wilful disobedience to God's Word by His people lay behind the problem; here the unequal yoke was occasioned by the successful evangelization of only one party in a marriage that was contracted by two unbelievers.

2. It is always possible because, those *professed* believers who refuse to heed church discipline, and persist in this refusal, at length are judged unbelievers (in a functional judgment that excludes them from the church) *because* of the failure to reach a peaceful settlement of differences.

can do no more (except pray, of course); he is *required* to do no more. This is true in law, in everyday interpersonal relationships and (as we shall see in I Cor. 7:12-16) in marriage. When dealing with unbelievers, then, there is a genuine possibility of a different outcome that may allow (require) a different response from the believer. That is why Paul distinguishes between the two groups contemplating divorce in I Corinthians 7. The outcomes of peace-making, leading toward reconciliation, may differ, calling for differing ultimate resolutions of the problems.[3]

Now, in the next chapter, let us turn our attention to some first comments on divorce among believers.

---

3. But, N.B., here (as in Rom. 12:18) *two* possible responses to the believer's peaceful overtures by unbelievers are in view. The Christian is to pursue peace and harmony always. When peace cannot be effected, the reason *must* lie in the unbeliever; failure must *never* be the believer's fault.

CHAPTER 8

Divorce Among Believers
(Preliminary Considerations)

Let us consider what Paul says to the first group that he addresses on the subject of divorce: believers married to believers. His words are found in I Corinthians 7:10, 11:

> To those who are married I give this authoritative instruction (not I but the Lord): A wife must not separate from her husband (but if she does indeed separate, she must remain unmarried or be reconciled to her husband); and a husband must not divorce his wife.

The basic, twofold command (and, note, it is that; it isn't merely good advice) in these verses is that neither the Christian wife nor the Christian husband may divorce one another. Thus, Paul teaches the same fundamental truth concerning Christians in marriage that Christ does (like Mark and Luke, and unlike Matthew, it suits Paul's purpose not to mention the exception clause, "except for sexual sin [*porneia*]"[1]). Temporarily, then, we may set aside a discussion of that exception and return to it later. For now (keeping that exception on the back burner) we may say with Paul (Mark and Luke) that Jesus forbade believers to divorce one another. That is the teaching of verses 10, 11. Let us now see exactly how Paul put it.

To begin with, notice that there is a command in verse 10 "a wife must not separate from her husband," followed by a balancing command to the husband (v. 11): "and a husband must not divorce her." This twofold command is without exception (as we said) because that is not in view here.

Now, Paul continues, "but if she does indeed separate . . ." (v. 11).[2] Why does he say that, and what does he have in mind? Certainly, as some wrongly suppose, he does not immediately contradict his command in verse 10, by allowing precisely what he has just explicitly said that Jesus forbids!

---

1. In this instance, Paul may have omitted the exception in order to set up the contrast between vv. 10, 11 and vv. 12-16 more sharply. Surely he understood the exception, but *here* it would not serve his general purpose to mention it. To do so would (unnecessarily) complicate what he wished to say.

2. *Chorizo* = separate by divorce. Paul may use this word as an echo of Jesus' use in Matt. 19:6; Mark 10:9. There it is clear also that *chorizo* refers to divorce.

Plainly, then, he has in view a further danger and is concerned to warn against it. The command not to separate by divorce (*chorizo*) stands; but (Paul says) if the wife disobeys this command (and presumably, this holds for the husband too) and *does* dissolve the marriage by divorce, she must remain unmarried (i.e., not marry another) so that she will be in a position at all times to repent and be reconciled to her husband. If she marries another, she pushes her disobedience one step beyond and gets herself into an irremediable situation (cf. Deut. 24:1-4).[3]

The first thing, then, is to see that Paul gives no permission to separate, but that in acknowledging the fact that divorce may occur because of sinful disobedience, he simply wants to warn against further complications arising out of additional sin.[4]

Now, notice that the word *separate* means "to separate by divorce."[5] The word clearly has this meaning both in the Gospels and here. In both, the "separation" leads to a state where the wife is said to be "unmarried"

---

3. There is good reason to think that Paul had Deut. 24:1-4 in mind when writing v. 11. After all, it was a discussion of Deut. 24 by Jesus and the Pharisees to which Paul refers in vv. 10, 11. Moreover, adultery occurs when one who is divorced, with obligations to be reconciled to and remarry his former spouse, instead marries another.

4. It also would be sin to marry another when one has obtained a divorce from a believer on unbiblical grounds. The believer is obligated to repent and reestablish the first marriage properly.

It is very important to recognize the problem of *obligations*. Counselors always must be very careful to check out obligations that remain. If a believer's obligation is to remain unmarried/be reconciled, he may have to say "No, you cannot marry another. You've never dealt with your obligations before God and your former spouse." Often churches don't handle such matters properly, so such cases will crop up. But regardless of what a church did or didn't do, now that a failure to assume some obligation has appeared, the believer must repent—even if it is now two or three years later— and do what should have been done at the time when the divorce was contemplated; obligations (sooner or later) must be met. All wrongs must be righted, as far as possible. Sure it is a can of worms; I agree with you. But if you help a counselee to remove and work on one worm at a time, eventually you'll have an empty can.

If in the course of doing so, it becomes necessary for the believer to pursue church discipline according to Matt. 18:15ff. and the church to which his/her spouse belongs refuses to exercise discipline when properly requested to do so, the believer (and, if necessary, the counselor at a later point) must point out that discipline is a right and privilege of the members of Christ's church, which is designed (among other things) to lead to reconciliation, and (as such) may not be withheld. If (after visits between pastors and [if necessary] church boards) the other church still refuses to exercise discipline, they should be treated (in a functional judgment) *as* unbelievers (just as a liberal church which also refuses to heed Christ's authority is) and the spouse who is a member there also. Then the whole matter falls into I Cor. 7:15. The matter should be pursued to the point of setting it to rest. An outline of the proceedings, together with the outcome, should be recorded in the church minutes. See the footnote on II Cor. 2:6-11 in *The Christian Counselor's New Testament*.

5. See two footnotes *supra*. Also, cf. comments on the biblical and extrabiblical uses of this word in the previous chapter (chap. 6).

(*agamos*): "let her remain unmarried," and where man reverses the yoking together of a man and woman that God effected in marriage.

There was nothing of our modern view of separating (legal or otherwise) as we know it—a leaving of one's marriage partner *without divorce*. All such separation is strictly forbidden in I Corinthians 7:5.

Why then is the divorced wife advised to remain *agamos* (unmarried)? Paul does not mean, let her remain in an unmarried state *per se*—i.e., not married to anyone, *including her husband* whom she has divorced. He is saying, stay unmarried *in relationship to all others*. Or, he says (better still), repent right away and remarry the man you wrongly left. Indeed, if she does remain unmarried for a space of time, it is *in order to allow for the possibility* of reconciliation. Marriage to another would preclude reconciliation.[6] What Paul is after is reconciliation; he wants these two believers to put the marriage back together in a new and more biblical way. Since all believers have the Word and the Spirit, they have all that they need to bring about not only a reconciliation, but—in the future—a marriage that sings!

Now, notice another important fact. Even when a separation by divorce occurs as the result of disobedience, that divorce—though sinful, though obtained on illegitimate grounds—broke the marriage. The grounds may be illegitimate; the divorce itself isn't. Believers who wrongly separate by divorce are said to be "unmarried." This point appears in all the Scriptures.

Just as a marriage is made by covenantal, contractual agreement, so too is it dissolved by the breaking of that agreement in divorce. It is quite wrong, then, to speak of divorced parties (even in this case) as "still married in God's sight." Here, as elsewhere (Deut. 24:1-4), God calls them "unmarried." The terminology, "still married in God's sight," is extrabiblical, unbiblical and harmful. It finds no support or counterpart anywhere in the Bible. Instead, in God's sight—if we are to believe the Holy Spirit's vocabulary—divorced persons are considered *agamos;* and that is how God deals with them. This terminology was selected not only to inform us but also to guide us in *our* dealings with one another. It is a serious matter to make God's Word of no effect by covering it over with our own teaching in phraseology that contradicts it.

The opposing view—that someone might still be married though divorced

---

6. In this case, it is not polyandry that is in view, but the idea that, since the divorce was in disobedience to God's command (v. 10), it falls into the situation covered by Deut. 24:1-4, where, even if a second husband were to divorce her, she would be prohibited from remarriage with her first husband.

—leads to many wrong ideas and acts on the part of the divorced parties and those counseling them. For instance (to mention but one), if one thinks two persons are married in God's sight (though divorced), he must therefore conclude that these parties still have marriage obligations including sexual obligations (I Cor. 7:3-5). Believing this, a Christian counselor would find himself in the position of urging his sinfully-divorced counselee(s) to continue to live together and to maintain regular sexual intercourse *after divorce*. He is not only advocating disobedience to the civil law, but (worse) if, as I believe him to be, he is wrong, he is advocating fornication. Sexual relations outside marriage are forbidden. God's Word knows nothing of any such irregular union. It is easy enough to freely throw around such phrases as "still married in God's eyes," but it is quite a serious matter to face up to their implications.

Indeed, the concept is repugnant. God has called the state of two sinfully-divorced believers *agamos* (unmarried). By our rationalizations, let us not put together what God has separated! The facts are plain—a divorce *does* break a marriage. Obligations belonging to marriage and rights and privileges of marriage do not pertain to divorced persons. Other obligations are placed upon sinfully-divorced parties, however:

1. They are required (again by command—I Cor. 7:11) to remain unmarried (i.e., not to marry another) in order to
2. be able to become reconciled.

Until they are remarried, all rights and privileges of marriage as well as all obligations of married persons, no longer pertain. Their chief obligation is reconciliation, and therefore all that leads to it. This matter must be understood thoroughly in order to deal with many cases.

Now, this point can be made not only from I Corinthians 7:10, 11, but from other passages as well. For example, when Jesus said, "Therefore, what God has yoked together nobody must separate"[7] (Matt. 19:6; Mark 10:9), He was not warning against an impossibility. The impact of His command would be lost entirely if—as some say—it is impossible to separate sinfully-separated believers because they are still married in God's sight.

Moreover, in Deuteronomy 24:1-4 (as we shall see when we look at this passage more thoroughly later on), the case in view involves a bill of divorce given for inadequate (and, therefore, sinful) reasons. Yet, when the wife leaves her first husband, she "becomes the wife of another" who is called

---

7. The word used in both gospels is *chorizo* = to separate by divorce.

43

her "husband" (vv. 2, 3). And, we read, the first man "may not take her again to be his wife" (v. 4). On the assumption that, though divorced, she is still her first husband's wife "in God's sight," when she married another she committed not only adultery[8] but bigamy in God's eyes. Yet, those words, "the wife of another," etc., say otherwise. If she is *another's* wife, she is no longer the first man's wife. She is not accused of bigamy (or polyandry). No, instead, we are told most plainly that the first man may not ever again take her "*to be* his wife" (v. 4). The language precludes the view that all along she was his wife anyway. She is forbidden to *become* his wife *again*. That obviously means that she isn't his wife after the divorce.[9]

All in all, I think that you must agree, the notion that one can be still married though divorced is a view that is without one shred of biblical support.[10] Rather, the view was designed to support an unbiblical position; it was not derived from the exegesis of biblical passages.

Now it is time to turn to the second possible divorce situation considered by Paul in I Corinthians 7: the contemplated divorce of a believer married to an unbeliever. I shall treat this matter fully in the next chapter.

---

8. We must discuss the meaning of adultery later on.

9. Surely if it forbids becoming a wife again merely in *man's* sight, while all along she remains his wife in God's eyes, a most remarkable situation arises: she may not ever do outwardly what is true inwardly. Any such notion is totally foreign to biblical teaching.

Moreover, if one holds that marriage to a second husband (rather than the divorce to the first) is what breaks the marriage, why did Jesus speak of divorce (separation) as what breaks God's yoke? He should have said that marriage to another does so. On this false view adultery = polyandry, but not polygamy.

10. To hold, with some, that Rom. 7:1-3 teaches that *nothing* can break a marriage but death (1) is a repudiation of Christ's words that man can put asunder by divorce what God has yoked together, (2) is to misunderstand the intent of Rom. 7 where marriage is not under discussion but is used illustratively only, (3) is to fail to recognize that for purposes of illustration the general principle is set forth without any qualifying exceptions as these would complicate and thus defeat the intent of the illustration, clouding Paul's point, and (4) is to call all remarriages after divorce polygamy or polyandry "in God's eyes."

CHAPTER 9

Divorce Among the Unequally Yoked

That there is a situation to which Jesus did not address Himself when speaking about divorce is clear from Paul's words in I Corinthians 7:12-16 (esp. v. 12). In verse 12 Paul says,

> To the rest I (not the Lord) say. . . .

By this statement, we have seen (in chap. 7) that Paul doesn't mean "I'm going to give an unauthoritative, uninspired opinion" (or anything of the sort), but (rather) "I'm about to take up an issue that Jesus did not discuss."[1]

The words, "to the rest" imply the existence of another group or class of persons to whom what was said in verses 10, 11 does not apply (at least in part). This second group differs from the first in that, unlike the group which Jesus discussed, this second group finds itself in a different situation, facing different problems.

Now that the church had moved out into the Mediterranean world, making Greek and Roman converts, frequently either a husband or a wife was saved while his/her marriage partner was not. This posed any number of problems (some of which are dealt with in I Pet. 3[2]), one of which had to do with divorce.

It is one thing to contemplate divorce with a believer (cf. chap. 7): there are resources (the Word and the Spirit) of which both parties may avail themselves, there is a mutually basic commitment to obey Christ and there is the process of church discipline that (in the last resort) may be activated if either one or the other (or both) refuses to deal with problems. There is, therefore, hope for that marriage and every reason for insisting upon reconciliation.

---

1. There are reasons for this:
    1. Jesus was speaking to persons in the covenant context of His church;
    2. He was responding to comments on Deut. 24:1-4, a passage regulating divorce among professed believers;
    3. He was concerned to reiterate the basic principles of marriage given to Adam.
   In other words, it was not Christ's purpose to cover all possible circumstances or every angle of the divorce question.
   2. For more on this, see my commentary on I Peter, *Trust and Obey* (Phillipsburg, N. J.: Presbyterian & Reformed Pub. Co., 1979).

But here is an entirely different situation—a believer contemplating divorce with his/her unbelieving spouse. None of the resources mentioned above are available to the unbeliever except the third, and the third resource (church discipline) is not available to the believer. Thus, there cannot be the same insistence on reconciliation; the same sort of hope does not exist. And, indeed, we do not see Paul *requiring* it.

Rather than commanding the believer not to divorce his unsaved partner regardless of what happens, he requires something less: he (or she) must not divorce a partner who is willing to make a go of their marriage. Indeed, the believer is told to do all he/she can to hold the marriage together for the sake of the unbelieving partner (hoping he/she will come to know Christ through continued association with the believer[3]) and for the sake of the children (who if taken out of the believer's care would be counted and treated as pagans—i.e., "unclean"[4]). But if, after all has been done by the believer to prevent it, the unbeliever does not agree to go on with the marriage, divorce is an acceptable alternative (v. 15).

Now, I have said all of this quickly and in a summary way, but let us go back over it again looking at several points more closely as we do.

In an earlier chapter, I have shown scripturally that, though permitted, divorce is never desirable. All divorces stem from sin, though not all divorces are sinful. Here too, in I Corinthians 7:12-16, divorce is not the ideal. Even for a mixed marriage, the goal is to continue the marriage if at all possible (what makes it not possible to do so I shall come to presently). Paul marshals powerful arguments (mentioned above) to convince believers that they must not divorce[5] their unbelieving partners, if their spouses wish to continue living with them. To these arguments he adds the flat statement that the believer *must* not divorce the unbeliever who consents to live with him. In accordance with the general principle in Romans 12:18, "if possible," the

---

3. To be "sanctified" by the believer (v. 14) means that the unbelieving partner is "set aside" to a "unique" position where he/she is exposed regularly to the gospel and the Holy Spirit's influences. It does not mean saved.

4. To be "holy" rather than "unclean" (v. 14) means that the child of a believer is "separated" from others by being placed under the care and discipline of God's church and is subject to many influences that others who are "unclean" (a word referring to gentiles or pagans) are not. God's care and discipline of these little ones in the flock truly sets them aside from others who are not in this privileged position. The child is not said to be saved.

5. The word used in vv. 12, 13 is *aphiemi*, which means, "to send away, divorce, leave." Either of the two basic senses is applicable; the believer is to do nothing to break up the marriage, but everything to preserve it.

believer must live "in peace" with his spouse.[6]

But, what if it isn't possible for the Christian (after doing all he/she can) to hold the marriage together? Suppose the unbeliever wants a divorce? Perhaps he says, "I didn't bargain for a wife like this when I married her. She won't lie for me any more, won't participate in any more wife-swapping parties, won't get drunk, reads her Bible . . . I've had it! I want out of this marriage!"[7]

Under circumstances where the unbeliever wants to get out of the marriage, Paul says, "let him separate" (v. 15). The clause (literally) reads, "if the unbeliever is separating [*chorizo* = to separate by divorce], let him separate [*chorizo*]." The words "is separating" (or, possibly, "separates") show not only that the unbeliever has divorce in mind, but (at the very least) has taken the step of plainly declaring that he/she wants to dissolve the marriage. The words indicate that there is some movement in that direction. (Today, steps like seeing a lawyer,[8] etc., might also be included). The Berkeley version catches the idea in the words when it translates,

In case the unbeliever wants to separate, let there be separation.

Here, the idea is that if the unbeliever is expressly desirous of separating (by divorce), the believer must not try to hinder him.[9] There is no limitation of this passage to divorce after desertion, although (clearly) desertion would be an act evidencing a strong desire to separate. It would plainly imply lack of consent over continuing the marriage (vv. 12, 13).

6. Many Christians want to get out of mixed marriages when their spouses have no such desire. This can be neither encouraged nor countenanced. Nor may Christians do anything to provoke their spouses to leave. Everything like that is contrary to the spirit of this passage.

7. But not only on such grounds. Paul gives no reasons for the unbeliever's desire to break up the marriage. The Christian is not restricted to certain grounds only. The permissive imperative "let him depart" applies to any case in which the unbeliever no longer wishes (or "agrees") to "live with" the believer (cf. vv. 12, 13)—regardless of what that reason may be (so long as the believer has not provoked him/her to it instead of trying to hold the marriage together).

8. No lawyer and no civil transaction were required in Paul's day.

9. In our culture, grounds for divorce are still required in some states. This creates problems. There is no biblical requirement for a divorce bill to state the grounds. It was simply a legal notice that the marriage had been dissolved. Today, unbelievers may try to obtain a divorce (in Paul's day, you didn't *obtain* it from the state; you simply *gave* it) on false grounds. The believer may not condone the lie, and, himself, may have to file suit for divorce on true grounds in order to comply with Paul's command, "Let him separate." The "no fault divorce"—devoid of grounds—though the motives behind it must be deplored, actually could be a blessing to Christians. The state never was competent to judge grounds for divorce. (Neither, the state nor lawyers can do exegesis.) No fault divorce will force the church to investigate and determine grounds; something she should be doing anyway and recording on her books.

47

So then, the general principle seems clear enough: where there is no consent (agreement) by the unbeliever to continue the marriage (vv. 12, 13) but (on the contrary) there is a desire to dissolve it, the Christian must not stand in the way of the separation. Paul uses a permissive imperative: "let him separate." This is a command; it is the one instance in which divorce is *required*.

There is in verse 15 both a description of the state of the believer after the divorce, and a reason appended to the command to "let him separate." Let us examine both.

1. The state in which the believer finds himself following such a divorce is defined: "Under these circumstances the brother or sister is not bound."

All the bonds of marriage have been removed. He is released entirely from every marriage obligation, and is a totally free person. Nor is there any obligation to be reconciled in marriage.[10] Paul expresses this idea later on in verse 27b when he speaks about being "*released* from a wife." The word *released* is *luo*, "to loose," which in verse 27 is set over against *deo* "to bind" (which is used of being bound to a wife). The word *deo* again appears in verse 39 with the same meaning.[11] However, in verse 15 the word translated "bound" is *douloo*, an even stronger term that means "to enslave." The idea is that when the bonds of marriage are broken, the believer is released from his marriage obligations to the unbeliever *and* from the burden of trying to maintain a marriage that the unbeliever doesn't want. He is released from this slavery.

2. The reason appended to the command is: "God has called you to peace."

This important consideration has been overlooked by a number of commentators. We must not do so, since it reaches to the bottom of the problem that Paul has in view. God doesn't want any loose ends dangling about a Christian's marriage; He wants problems in marriage resolved. He wants peace. Either there is to be a marriage or there isn't; God will

---

10. Clearly, the believer could not remarry the unbelieving partner (unless he/she should become a Christian) since to do so would violate another biblical command to marry "only in the Lord" (v. 39). A believer must not marry an unbeliever, even if the unbeliever is a former spouse!

11. *Deo* also is used in Matt. 16:18; 18:18 in the formula for binding and loosing as it is in its Hebrew counterpart, *ashar*.

not settle for something in-between. That simply will not do. The matter must be set to rest one way or the other so that there will be *peace*.

Too often Christians, on bad advice, have settled for the in-between. Let me describe it. Believing (wrongly) that she must remain married to her unbelieving husband, no matter what, a Christian woman holds on even when her husband wants to end their marriage. He, then, may begin running around with other women (if he hasn't been doing so already) and at length may even desert her. Yet, urged on by bad counsel, she will not agree to a divorce. He may stay away from home for six month periods at a time, occasionally showing up for a week or so. This upsets the kids and the life of the home (hopes are aroused and shattered). His wife may get pregnant (if married, she must agree to sex if he seeks it), and so it goes on and on. She is always hoping against hope, yet there is no evidence at all of a desire on his part to consent to a marriage. She may hang on for years; for life!

There is nothing peaceful about that! Everything is constantly being upset; nothing is settled. There is nothing but loose ends. God wants the matter to be concluded so that (in one way or the other) there will be peace—the resolution of the matter. This is an important principle.

Today's view of separation-rather-than-divorce is patently unbiblical because it violates this principle. It settles nothing, but keeps everything up in the air, and militates against true peace.[12] This wicked substitute for the biblical solution (peace by reconciliation or by divorce) fights against true peace. All is held in limbo. It deceives by its temporary sense of relief, (often mistaken for peace). But nothing is settled (made truly peaceful) by it.

Christians frequently have resorted to separation rather than divorce thinking it to be the lesser of two evils. But, because it is a human substitute for the biblical options, separation-instead-of-divorce does more harm than good. Counselors will tell you that in most instances where separation has occurred, it is much harder to effect a reconciliation than when it has not. It isn't easy to bring people together again when you have encouraged (or permitted) them to separate; in separation not only do they experience a false sense of peace, but they learn not to face and deal with problems in order to solve them. God wants resolution of difficulties, not the avoidance of them.

Modern separation is often described as a "cooling off period."

---

12. There is an initial release of tension that gives a temporary false sense of peace, and that makes the parties reluctant to come together again.

Unless one has in mind a couple of hours or (at most) a couple of days for cooling off *in order to face more coolly and resolve difficulties,* he is talking about something utterly unbiblical.

So, we have seen that there is only one case in which, when all else has failed, a believer is required to separate by divorce from his unbelieving spouse. We must turn now to the one instance when a believer *may* separate by divorce from another believer. But, unlike this present instance, he is never *required* to do so.

CHAPTER 10

The Exceptional Clause

We have seen already that while God did not institute divorce, He (nevertheless) *regulated it*. I shall look at that point again in chapter 11. We discovered that God hates divorce, not as a process but because of its sinful causes and many of its devastating consequences. All divorces, in one way or another, are caused by sin; but not all divorces are sinful. In the last chapter, for instance, we examined a case in point—the divorce of a mixed couple (believer/unbeliever). The Bible legitimized such a divorce after every attempt had been made by the believer to maintain the marriage to his unbelieving spouse. But if that spouse adamantly refuses to go on with the marriage, he is *required* not to stand in the way of a divorce (I Cor. 7:15). This divorce is reluctantly granted after all attempts to avert it have failed. The effect of that divorce, we noted, was to free the believer of all marriage obligations as well as any obligation to remarry that unbelieving former spouse. He is free to remarry another.

Now, we turn to the exceptional clause in Matthew, chapters 5 and 19, by which Jesus made it plain that there is *one* ground on which believers might divorce a spouse—fornication (or sexual sin). In this case, however, no requirement to divorce the other is laid down. Note well, at the outset, that Jesus acknowledged one, and only one, ground for divorce among believers: *porneia* ("fornication," or "sexual sin").

I shall not discuss why it is that Paul in I Corinthians 7:10, 11, and Mark and Luke in their Gospels, all omit the exceptional clause (I have already commented on Paul's omission, and comments on Mark and Luke would be even more speculative). Perhaps what is much more important is to note that Matthew *does* include it twice. Let us ask why?

Matthew's Gospel was written for Jews. And, as the records of the controversy over divorce among the Jews (both within the Bible and in other sources) shows, there were many in the camp of Hillel who held that a divorce might be given for "any cause."[1] (We shall look at this matter more

---

1. Cf. Matt. 19:3. Hillel's followers contended that the words "some unseemly thing" in Deut. 24 permitted divorce for such minor reasons as spoiling a meal, and that surely one might divorce his wife if he found another woman whom he preferred (cf. *Gittin* 14:10). Cf. also Josephus, *Antiquities* 4:23 (Josephus divorced his wife because he was "displeased at her behavior," *Life*, p. 75).

fully when we examine the teaching of Jesus in the light of Deut. 24:1-4.)

For now, however, let us be content to consider the exceptional clause itself. Matthew is careful to include this clause because *he wants to restrict divorce* among Jewish converts. Contrary to fears of some today, who think that allowing divorce for fornication is a serious loosening of Christian morals, Matthew saw the effect of the inclusion of this exceptional clause in exactly the opposite light. By pointing out Christ's *only* exception, he knew that for many this would have a tightening effect on morality in the church. It is instructive that Matthew's inclusion of the passage that follows (Matt. 19:10ff.) demonstrates precisely that sort of reaction by the disciples (who were probably representative of others in their society):

> The disciples said to Him, "If that is the way that it must be between a man and his wife, it would be better not to marry"[2] (Matt. 19:10).

Obviously, the response by the disciples indicates that the one-and-only exception, in their culture at that time, would be taken as a severe restriction upon divorce practices.

Now, to the clause in detail. Let us look at it in its two forms:

1. ". . . except on the ground [or for the cause] of sexual sin [fornication, *porneia*]" (Matt. 5:32).
2. ". . . except for sexual sin [fornication, *porneia*]" (Matt. 19:9).

The form of the clause differs in the two places in which it appears, but the intent and basic content of each is the same. Probably, there is a more formal response in Matthew 19:3 (where Christ's *logos*="ground," answers to the Pharisees' *aitia*="cause" or "reason"). Fortunately, there is no problem regarding the textual evidence for these clauses, and hardly anyone disputes their genuineness.

But all sorts of other problems regarding the clauses have arisen; these (largely) have to do with matters of interpretation. For instance, some have wondered whether the exception extends not only to divorce, but also to remarriage. Again, some have seized on the word *porneia* (fornication, sexual sin) and argued that the clause refers to the dissolution of an engagement but not a marriage.

Let us consider first whether the exceptional clause refers to the remarriage as well as to the divorce. The answer is yes. There is no way of separating the two ideas in Matthew 19:9 or in Matthew 5:32. In the former passage, Jesus says that one commits adultery by marrying another unless he

---

2. N.B., they know that Jesus is speaking of married persons, not engaged ones.

has divorced his previous wife for fornication. That is the whole point of the statement about adultery. Moreover, in the latter, the divorced wife and her second husband are warned that they will commit adultery unless she was divorced for fornication.[3] Like it or not—and some don't—that is what Christ said. I shall not discuss this matter in more detail since John Murray has treated it so fully (and adequately) in his book.[4]

For here, let me but quote two summary statements by Murray:

> In other words, it must be observed that in this sentence as it stands no thought is complete without the principal verb, *moichatai* ["commits adultery"]. It is this committing adultery that is the ruling thought in this passage and it is quite indefensible to suppress it.[5]

And,

> The subject dealt with, therefore, is putting away and remarriage in coordination, and this coordination must not be disturbed in any way.[6]

The argumentation leading to those conclusions is solid and convincing.

Fornication and Adultery

In order to respond to the second objection—that the use of the word *fornication* indicates that Jesus spoke of the *dissolution of an engagement*, not a marriage—we must consider (among other things) the meaning of the terms fornication (*porneia*) and adultery (*moichao*)[7]. Some, to be sure, equate the two, thinking that they are used interchangeably. But a careful study of the use of these words both in the OT and NT Scriptures (including the usage of the Septuagint) reveals that there is a clear distinction between them. *Fornication* refers to sexual sin of any and all sorts; *adultery* is unfaithfulness toward one's marriage partner.

That there is confusion about the word *fornication* is understandable. In

---

3. Additional problems here must be considered later.

4. John Murray, *Divorce* (Philadelphia: Presbyterian and Reformed Publishing Co., 1961), pp. 35ff. See Murray's complete study.

5. Ibid., p. 40.

6. Ibid., p. 41.

7. The distinct Hebrew terms are *zahnah* (to commit fornication) and *nahaph* (to commit adultery). Of *zahnah*, Gesenius (Tregelles) says, "Attributed properly and chiefly to a woman; whether married . . . or unmarried, Gen. 38:24; Lev. 19:29; Hos. 3:3 . . . *min* is put before the husband *from* whom the adulteress departs in committing whoredom, *against* whom she transgresses, Psa. 73:27 . . . Hos. 1:2 . . . Hos. 4:12, and . . . Ezek. 23:5 . . . Ezek. 16:15 (she committed adultery [committed fornication] *with* a husband; i.e., whilst she had a husband . . .)," (Grand Rapids: Wm. B. Eerdmans, 1978), p. 249. Note that in Judg. 19:2, a concubine is said to commit fornication (*zahnah*) *against* her husband (she is called a "wife").

American law, the word *fornication* has come to mean sexual sin by unmarried persons, over against *adultery* which means sexual sin involving a married person. However, *that distinction must not be read back into the Bible* as many unwittingly do. It was not the biblical distinction. Indeed, Scripture writers used the word fornication (*porneia*) to describe *sexual sin in general,* and in the Bible it referred to cases of incest (I Cor. 5:1), homosexuality (Jude 7) and even adultery (Jeremiah 3:1, 2, 6, 8—here a married adulteress is divorced because of her fornication; cf. vv. 2, 6 in the LXX) as *fornication.*[8]

The interesting fact about the word *adultery* is that it has reference always to more than sexual sin. The marriage covenant is always in view. In addition to the notion of sexual unfaithfulness, adultery refers to the violation of the covenant of companionship by the introduction of another party into the picture. This third party appears on the scene in order to provide companionship (usually, if not always, of a sexual nature) instead of the wife or husband "of one's youth."

One of the most interesting joint occurences of the two words is found in *Sirach* 23:22, 23. There, this is said about an unfaithful wife: ". . . *en porneia emoicheuthe* "("she has committed adultery by fornication"). By engaging in sexual sin, she violated her covenant commitment to her husband.

Though some equate adultery and fornication, it is altogether wrong to do so. Frequently one hears the exceptional clause misquoted: "except for adultery." But, as we have seen, that is wrong. While in the context of Matthew 5, 19, adultery is in one's mind as he reads the exceptional clause, the clause itself does not place the emphasis (at that point) upon the effect of sexual sin (adultery), but upon the sin itself—the act by which one violates his marriage covenant. In both Matthew 5 and 19, Jesus' permission to divorce a spouse is based on the violating act (sexual sin, *porneia*) not on its effect (adultery).[9]

Why does Jesus focus on the act? Because He wants to cover all the possibilities. He declares fornication (sexual sin) to be the ground upon which one may serve a bill of divorce because fornication covers incest, bestiality, homosexuality and lesbianism as well as adultery. To speak of

---

8. Cf. Rev. 2:20, 23. In I Cor. 10:8, 23,000 persons are said to have committed fornication. Were all unmarried; did only unmarried persons engage in sexual sin? See also the use of *porneia* in the *LXX* at Ezek. 16:23; Hos. 2:3, 5; Amos 7:17. These, and other passages (some to be mentioned later on) demonstrate the true biblical use of *porneia* (Heb. *zahnah*).

9. Later, in the passages, He does (indeed) say something about adultery. But, N.B., in both passages the two terms are used consistently and carefully distinguished.

adultery only, might tend to narrow the focus too much.

Most modern translations translate *porneia* by words like "sexual sin," thus avoiding much of the confusion. All the sexual sins condemned as fornication are included.

The Engagement Thesis

Some, erroneously, have taught (and even teach widely today) that since Jesus used the word fornication, He was speaking about sexual sin during the engagement period; not after marriage. But, as we have seen already (and will see once again in this chapter and in the next), this view stems from a serious misunderstanding of the biblical use of *porneia*. The idea that divorce is allowed after engagement, but not after marriage cannot be sustained.[10] In addition to and including some reasons for rejecting the view:

1. Jesus and the Pharisees were not discussing engagement but marriage.
2. The passages about which Jesus and the Pharisees spoke (Gen. 2; Deut. 24:1-4) do not refer to engagement but to marriage.
3. We have shown (and will continue to demonstrate biblically) that the word *porneia* was used to speak of sexual sin leading to adultery as its effect.
4. We have shown that divorce was permitted to married persons (I Cor. 7:15).
5. In Deuteronomy 22:13-19; 22:28, 29, two cases are mentioned in which, *as a penalty,* the persons involved were forbidden to ever divorce their wives for any cause. But the entire point of the passage is lost if no one else could ever divorce his wife either. It is no penalty if true of everyone. The existence of such a penalty *demands* acceptance of the view that God recognized the possibility of legitimate divorce after marriage. Without that assumption, these verses in Deuteronomy 22 are meaningless.
6. In Ezekiel 23:1-9, God tells the story of two women who married Him (v. 4). They committed fornication both before and *after* marriage (cf. vv. 3, 5, 7, 8, 11, 14, 17, 19, 29, 30, 37, 43, 45, 46). Adultery is the effect of this fornication. In verse 5 we read, "Oholah committed sexual sin (fornication) under Me." The expression "under Me" means while under My authority and headship as her Husband (cf. the use of this expression in Num. 5:19, 20, 29). And in verse 29, we read "and the nakedness of your *adulteries* will be bared, even your lewdness and your *fornication*" (note the obvious connection of the terms in question[11]). Here is, again, a case of

---

10. The Talmud clearly speaks of divorce after engagement and divorce after marriage *Gittin* 18b. So, the cultural tradition is clear.

11. Lewdness and fornication describe the manner of committing adultery.

adulteries by fornication. The engagement thesis will not fit into this use of terminology.

7. God Himself divorced Israel for adulterous fornication. The passage in Jeremiah 3:1-8 is powerful; it utterly devastates the divorce-during-engagement theory. Here is what we read in verse 8:

> . . . for all the adulteries which faithless Israel had done, I sent her away and gave her a bill. (Berkeley)

Plainly, God knows what adultery and fornication are, always uses the terms properly and does not try to confuse us. If God says that He divorced Israel, pictured as a woman married to Him, for sinful adulteries, then His use of terms makes it clear that married persons can be legitimately divorced.

As I said, these reasons are not exhaustive, but they are compelling. The engagement theory has no support in the Scriptures and, indeed, the usage of the entire Bible annihilates it. The popularity of teachers who may espouse the theory is no basis for its acceptance.

So, it should be apparent by now that there is good reason for the standard, historical Protestant interpretation that, for fornication, a believer may divorce his spouse.

Note, however, that I say *may*. The Bible does not *require* divorce in such cases; divorce is *permitted*. It is clear that a husband or wife may forgive the sinning partner upon repentance. Indeed, in most cases of this sort, the biblical counselor will seek to bring the guilty party to repentance and then seek to bring about a reconciliation. If the guilty spouse repents, his partner must forgive him (cf. Luke 17:3ff).

Forgiveness involves not raising the matter again.[12] It is not possible for a believer to proceed to divorce after granting forgiveness.[13] Forgiveness also

---

12. Cf. extensive comments on repentance and (especially) forgiveness in my book, *More than Redemption* (Phillipsburg: Presbyterian and Reformed Publishing Co., 1979). When God forgives, He promises, "Your sin . . . will I remember against you no more."

13. Even if forgiveness could be separated from reconciliation (an unbiblical idea; in God's forgiveness, reconciliation and a new relationship always follow repentance and forgiveness—cf. the chart, and the discussion surrounding it, in *More than Redemption*, p. 213), it is impossible in our culture to obey the government, which requires parties to go to law to obtain a divorce (in biblical times you didn't *get* a divorce from the state, you *gave* a bill of divorce to your spouse—the government did not get involved), and to obey the Scriptures which forbid Christians to sue one another at law (I Cor. 6:1-8). Rather, I Cor. 6 obligates two Christians (even husbands and wives) to work out their problems before the church. That means that Matt. 18:15ff. must be followed. If one of the parties at length refuses to be reconciled, and he/she eventually is excommunicated, the other party may (*must*) treat him/her "as a heathen and a publican" (a functional judgment) and may proceed to law against that party for adulterous fornication or for reasons growing out of I Cor. 7:15 (for which, see chap. 9).

leads to a new relationship with the forgiven one. Divorce of a believing spouse who has committed fornication must, therefore, be restricted to those who refuse to repent of their sin.

But what about the situation in which the one who has been wronged wants to forgive (has done so in his heart in prayer before God), wants to go on with the marriage, but cannot yet *grant* forgiveness to the offender because he/she persists in sin, or (at least) will not repent and seek forgiveness (remember, Luke 17:3ff. speaks of granting forgiveness to those who *repent*).

In such cases, the reconciliation/discipline dynamic comes into play. Let me quote extensively, in this regard, from my book, *The Christian Counselor's Manual,* pp. 60-62.

As a concrete example of the crucial nature of the reconciliation/discipline dynamic, let us consider the growing problem of divorce among Christians. This is a problem with which every Christian pastor increasingly will find himself confronted. John Murray sketches several situations in the back of his landmark book, *Divorce,* as paradigms for handling practical cases.[14] They are helpful, but limited in use. A pastor soon discovers that there are many situations that do not fit into the framework of these paradigms. However, the addition of one further factor to what Murray has said so well about marriage and divorce will bring such problem cases within their framework and will enable counselors to bring every case to a successful conclusion. This factor is the reconciliation/discipline dynamic.

. . . .

The problem remains, however, as to what must be done when two professing Christians fail to keep their marriage together and reconciliation does not take place. Let us say that a husband who is a professing Christian refuses to be reconciled to his wife. If she continues to insist upon reconciliation (according to Matthew 18), but fails in her attempts at private confrontation, she must take one or two others from the church and confront her husband. Suppose she does and that he also refuses to hear them. In that case she is required to submit the problem officially to the church, which ultimately may be forced, by his adamant refusal to be reconciled, to excommunicate him for contumacy. Excom-

At any time that a believer engages a lawyer to discuss divorce proceedings, he/she is out of line with the Bible and should be told so. The church should step in immediately and, in accordance with I Cor. 6, should offer its services to help work out the difficulties that led to this action. Too often the church waits; sometimes lawyers, like some bad counselors, even encourage divorce (or separation) as a (supposed) solution to marital problems. Christians having difficulty do not need the added confusion that may generate. The church always gets first crack at solving problems—as God set things up.

14.   John Murray, *Divorce* (Philadelphia: Presbyterian and Reformed Publishing Company, 1961).

munication, Christ says, changes his status to that of a heathen and a publican, i.e., someone outside of the church (Matthew 18:17). Now he must be treated "*as* a heathen and a publican."[15] That means, for instance, that after reasonable attempts to reconcile him to the church and to his wife, he may be taken to court (I Corinthians 6:1-8 forbids *brethren* to go to law against one another[16]) to sue for a divorce (only, of course, if the excommunicated one deserts his partner).

By following the reconciliation dynamic, hopefully there will be reconciliation in most cases.[17] Whenever the principles of biblical reconciliation are followed faithfully, discipline rarely reaches the highest level of excommunication. Most marriages not only can be saved, but by proper help may be changed *radically* for good.[18] But in those few cases where reconciliation is refused, the believer who seeks it is not left in a state of limbo. He has a course of action to pursue, and if it leads to excommunication and desertion he is no longer obligated to remain married indefinitely.[19] This is true only if the believer's marriage partner during the whole process of discipline has failed to demonstrate evidence of repentance and faith, if that partner has been excommunicated, and if he (or she) wishes to dissolve the marriage. Continued rejection of the help and authority of Christ and His church finally leads to excommunication.

An excommunicated party who continues to be unrepentant must be looked upon and treated as a heathen and publican. He shows no signs of a work of grace. When he has been put outside of the church and still evidences no signs of salvation, the believing partner may deal with him as with an unbeliever. This means that if he leaves the believer under those circumstances, the latter is no longer under "bondage." The word in I Corinthians 7:21ff. governing the relationship of a believer to an unbelieving marriage partner then comes into effect. By plugging in the reconciliation/discipline dynamic to the marriage-divorce-remarriage problem, the solution to ninety-nine percent of these cases that heretofore may have seemed unsolvable immediately may be seen. Most parties hopefully will come to reconciliation, but those who will

---

15. The force of *hosper* is "treat him as." William F. Arndt and F. Wilbur Gingrich (Chicago: The University of Chicago Press, 1951), p. 908.

16. This fact is important. A church trial leading to excommunication must always precede any civil trial, since civil trials between believers are explicitly forbidden. This means that hasty action is slowed down and a process aimed at reconciliation not only is begun, but must run its full course unsuccessfully *before* legal proceedings may be begun. Thus Christians are afforded ample opportunity to consider the consequences of their actions before taking further action that might precipitously bring about new and greater evils.

17. This is to be expected among Christians. Cf. Proverbs 14:9 (T.E.V.).

18. Often the weld is stronger than the metal before the break.

19. Often refusal to be reconciled leading to excommunication ends in separation from bed and board or desertion.

not repent and be reconciled should be disciplined. Either way, matters are not left at loose ends. [20]

In the next chapter, we shall peruse the Gospel record of Christ's words about divorce and the passages upon which His comments are based.

20. It is of vital importance for the church to pronounce judgment officially whenever cases of discipline have been adjudicated, *even when they have been settled by reconciliation.* The fact of settlement should be noted on the minutes of the board of elders. This is important for the sake of the parties involved so that in years to come they always may be able to refer back to the pronouncement of the church that the matter was closed satisfactorily.

CHAPTER 11 Christ, Deuteronomy and Genesis

The passages that we shall consider now are Genesis 2; Deuteronomy 24:1-4; Matthew 5:31, 32; 19:3-9; Mark 10:2-12 and Luke 16:18. The two OT and two basic NT passages come together in a very interesting way in Christ's teaching about divorce.

The passage in Deuteronomy was introduced by the Pharisees, and by Jesus, quoting them. Genesis 2 was brought into the discussions in order to remind His listeners of the original basis, goals and purposes of marriage, and that divorce was not included among them; divorce reluctantly was introduced (not by God or even by Moses—who only permitted and regulated it—but) by men later on as a result of their hardhearted (stubborn) attitudes toward their spouses and God's law. By bringing the Genesis passage into the picture, Jesus set the whole discussion into its proper context.

In the interplay of these various passages, including Christ's comments, we find that Jesus answered a number of the questions that are regularly raised about divorce. But right there lies a difficulty—interpretation of Jesus' interpretations is not uniform. One reason seems to be a failure to relate these passages properly. In this chapter, I shall try to interpret them in relationship to one another.

But first, read the verses through in their entirety.

> Then God said: Let Us make man in Our image, after Our likeness, and let them bear rule over the fish in the sea, over the birds of the air, over the animals; over the whole earth and over all creeping things that crawl on the earth. So God created man in His image; in the image of God He created him; male and female He created them. God blessed them; God said to them: Be fruitful; multiply; fill the earth and subdue it; bear rule over the fish of the sea; over the birds of the air and over every living, moving creature on earth. . . . The Lord God said: It is not good for the man to be alone; I will make him a suitable helper, completing him. . . . So the Lord God caused a deep sleep to overcome Adam, and as he slept He took one of his ribs and filled up the place with flesh. From the rib He had taken from the man, God formed a woman and brought her to the man. Adam said, "This at last is bone of my bones and flesh of my flesh; she shall be called Woman because she was taken

out of a man." For this reason a man shall leave his father and his mother and cling to his wife and they shall become one flesh. Both the man and his wife were naked and they felt no shame in each other's presence (Gen. 1:26-28; 2:18, 21-25, Berkeley).

"When a man has married a wife and comes to dislike her, having found something improper in her, and he writes her a bill of divorce and, putting it in her hand, sends her from his house, and she goes off and becomes the wife of another, and her second husband, likewise comes to hate her and also gives her a bill of divorce and sends her away, or if the second husband dies, in such case, the man who first divorced her, may not take her again to be his wife, for she has been defiled; such practice is abhorrent to the LORD, and you must not bring such guilt upon the land which the LORD your God is giving you for your heritage" (Deut. 24:1-4, Berkeley).

"It was also said, 'Whoever divorces his wife should give her a divorce certificate.' But I tell you that anyone who divorces his wife, except for unfaithfulness, makes her commit adultery, and whoever marries a divorced woman commits adultery. . . ." Then the Pharisees approached Him to test Him. They asked, "Is it right to divorce one's wife for every given reason?" He replied, "Have you not read that from the beginning the Creator made them male and female, and said, On this account a man shall leave his father and mother and be joined to his wife, and the two shall be one flesh?' So they are no longer two but one flesh. What God then has joined, man must not separate." They said to Him, "Why then did Moses command to give a divorce certificate and to dismiss her?" He answered them, "Due to your hard-heartedness Moses permitted you to divorce your wives, but it was not that way from the beginning. I tell you that whoever divorces his wife, except for unfaithfulness, and marries another commits adultery" (Matt. 5:31, 32; 19:3-9, CCNT).

And there came Pharisees questioning Him, "Is it lawful for a man to divorce his wife?"—testing Him. He answered them, "What ruling did Moses give you?" They said, "Moses permitted the writing of a divorce certificate and to divorce her." Jesus told them, "In view of your hardheartedness he wrote you this ruling, but from the beginning, from the time of creation male and female He made them; 'Therefore shall a man leave his father and mother and shall cling to his wife; and the two shall be one flesh'; so that they are no longer two but one flesh. What God therefore has joined, let not man divide." When they were indoors the disciples questioned Him again on that subject, and He told them, "Whoever divorces his wife and marries another, commits adultery against her, and if she divorces her husband and marries another, she commits adultery" (Mark 10:2-12, CCNT).

"Whoever divorces his wife and marries another, commits adultery; and he who marries the divorcee commits adultery" (Luke 16:18, CCNT).

Consider Deuteronomy 24:1-4. Notice that, like all modern versions, the Berkeley translation is different from the King James. It takes verses 1-3 as the protasis (the section with the if and when conditional clauses that contain the supposition) and verse 4 as the apodosis (the section with the concluding clause that contains the statement—here a regulation—that is based on the supposition). The King James takes only the first half of verse 1 as the protasis. This important difference results in understanding Moses to teach that if a man divorces his wife for a cause other than fornication, if she remarries and is divorced again (or her second husband dies), *then* (the rule *now* follows), the first husband may not remarry because she would be defiled. Fortunately, all commentators agree on this change.[1]

Note, in Deuteronomy 24:1-4, there is no command to divorce, no criteria for determining what is a valid or invalid divorce, nor even a requirement to give a bill of divorce. (Moses mentions the proper legal process with its three steps not to institute the process, or even to insist upon it, but rather to make it clear that what he is speaking about is a genuine divorce proceeding.) Thus,

1. Deuteronomy 24 merely recognizes divorce as an existing, legal process that it regulates.
2. Deuteronomy 24 does not institute or even allow divorce for a cause other than fornication. This is an important point that I shall expand presently.
3. Deuteronomy 24 does not encourage easy divorce; indeed, the whole point of the four verses in question is to forestall hasty action by making it impossible to rectify the situation when divorce and remarriage to another takes place (cf. I Cor. 7:11).

What is the import of Deuteronomy 24:1-4? It *recognizes* divorce and *regulates* it—in *one* particular.

In the four verses under consideration, Moses takes up a particular case [2] (just described) and in order to eliminate the practice of easy divorce and remarriage that evidently prevailed in the surrounding pagan culture (and that also may have been becoming prevalent among God's people) puts an end to capricious action of the sort. "If I'm wrong, I'll just remarry Mary, if and when she becomes available again or if I can induce her to leave her second husband and return to me" was the way some were thinking. No! says Moses in this passage. "You'd better think twice before you divorce her, because if you can't get her to remarry you before she marries another,

---

1. Argumentation for it can be found in most of the standard commentaries.
2. Cf. the formula, "If [or when] a man. . . " (v. 1) with 22:22, 25, 28; 24:5, 7, etc.

you will have lost the opportunity to do so *forever*," says Moses.

Now, about that much most interpreters seem to agree. But there is another matter that has caused some difficulty. As a matter of fact, it was already the occasion for problems as early as the time of Christ. I am referring, of course, to the words translated in the Berkeley version as "something improper." It is because of the something "improper" that the first husband "comes to dislike" his wife and ultimately divorces her.

The Hebrew words are *erwath dabar*. They have been translated in any number of ways, including, "something indecent," "something shameful," "some indecency," etc. Literally, the two Hebrew words are "a matter of nakedness." They seem to mean something indecent, disgusting or repulsive. Almost all interpreters agree with John Murray when he says:

> . . . there is no evidence to show that *erwath dabar* refers to adultery or an act of sexual uncleanness. . . . We may conclude that *erwath dabar* means some indecency or impropriety of behavior.[3]

The same expression is used, interestingly, in the twenty-third chapter of Deuteronomy (vv. 12-14). In that passage the Israelites were required to designate a place outside their camp as a toilet. There they were to have all their bowel movements, covering these with dirt by the use of a spade. The reason given is this:

> "The Lord your God walks among you to deliver you, to give you the victory, and your entire camp must be dedicated, so that He may see nothing indecent [*erwath dabar*] anywhere, so as to withdraw from you" (Berkeley).

Obviously, the use of this phrase here, in such close connection with chapter 24, should have a strong influence on the interpretation that we give it. How is it used? Clearly, *erwath dabar* has no reference to sexual sin in Deuteronomy 23. Rather, the matter of excrement mentioned gives direction about its import. The idea of repulsiveness or repugnancy seems uppermost.[4] The camp was to be kept free from anything that might be repulsive to God; it was to be clean and attractive because of His presence.

But what does *erwath dabar* refer to in Deuteronomy 24 if not to sexual sin? It is hard to say. The phrase is rather general and seems to cover anything and everything (in this case) a husband might deem repugnant, and

---

3. Op. cit., p. 12. See also Murray's arguments against understanding this expression to refer to sexual sin.

4. Notice how the Lord Himself would be repulsed ("so as to withdraw from you") by their lack of reverence toward Him if they allowed excrement to be strewn in His pathway as He walked about the camp.

that he might come to "dislike" [lit., "not find favor"] in his wife, so that he might determine to divorce her.

"But," you reply, "that would seem to imply that the Pharisees, who followed Hillel in saying that a man could divorce his wife 'for any reason' or 'on any ground' (Matt. 19:3), were correct, and that these followers of Shammai who restricted the grounds of divorce to fornication were wrong. If that is true, it would seem also to place Jesus on the wrong side of the issue—and we know that cannot be."

The answer to the objection is both a yes and a no. It is true that the use of the phrase in Deuteronomy 24:1-4 is sufficiently indefinite to cover almost anything that one might happen to find repulsive in his spouse. On that score, the disciples of Hillel in his liberal views on divorce were correct—but *only* on that single issue. The very difficulty that interpreters have had ever since in trying to nail down some more precise meaning to the phrase attests to the fact. Let's face the truth—the words are vague. But, of course these words are vague; that's the very point!

The phrase *erwath dabar* covers everything to which a husband might take offense short of *porneia* (sexual sin). But—and here is where we must immediately part company with Hillel—since the protasis (conditional section) does not command action or even approve of it (but only describes a possibility) these liberal Pharisees were quite wrong in concluding that the passage gives license to divorce for any cause.

Let's make that clear. It is one thing to say that the Bible says that a person might happen to commit murder; however, it is quite another to conclude, therefore that he *may* do so. But that is what Hillel and company had done. Because Moses spoke of the *possibility* of a man divorcing his wife for any cause (because of something repulsive to him), Hillel concluded that Moses permitted him to do so. Further, in taking this position, emphasis was shifted from the dangers of light views of divorce to properly giving a bill of divorce as the only consideration in divorcing another. The true emphasis—forestalling hasty divorces for insufficient causes—was lost sight of.

No, we must conclude, first of all, that (with Hillel) Moses was talking about (but certainly not approving, commanding or even permitting) believers divorcing their spouses for any cause other than sexual sin, the one ground that Jesus viewed as adequate. The vagueness of the expression *erwath dabar* is the very point to be noted. It does cover anything (short of fornication) that the husband might deem displeasing or repugnant.

In other words, I am saying that Deuteronomy 24:1-4 refers (as does I Cor. 7:10, 11—with which it has affinities, as we have seen) to a divorce given on unbiblical (or illegitimate) grounds. Such a divorce is legally proper but sinful. How do we know this? There are several reasons for reaching this conclusion. But there is one that is principal.

Note that in Deuteronomy 24:4, the wife may not remarry her first husband because she is "defiled" by the second marriage. Her divorce from the first man could not have been biblically acceptable even though it may have been formally valid. If it had been proper, and not sinful, that divorce would have freed her to marry the second man without sin. She would have had no obligation to remain married or be reconciled to her first husband. But the second marriage "defiled" her[5] (cf. Jer. 3:1; 23:11, 14, 15). We know that she was defiled by the second marriage and not by the second divorce because even if she was freed from the second husband by death, rather than by divorce (v. 3), her first husband is forbidden to marry her because of her defilement.

That this defilement lay not merely in the fact that the wife had entered into sexual relations with the second man, but rather in the violation of a covenantal agreement (the marriage contract) seems evident. Adultery was involved.

David took Michal back as his wife even though Saul had given her to another. This act was not condemned as an "abomination" and Michal was not considered defiled. The reason for the difference is that Michal was taken away by Saul; David did not divorce her for an inadequate, unbiblical reason.[6] The wrong, then, was not in the simple succession of men having the wife of Deuteronomy 24 (or David would have been forbidden Michal) but in the *manner* in which or the reasons for which the succession took place. What is contemplated and forbidden in Deuteronomy 24 that Jehovah calls an abomination and that leads to defilement has to do with more than the mere succession (which was identical to that of David and Michal). God would not have the land into which they were entering filled with the practice that he condemns so roundly in Deuteronomy 24. The wife of Deuteronomy 24, then, was not defiled by sexual relations with the second husband,[7] but by her involvement in marriage and sexual relations because of a divorce (though legal) that was sinful. Because the divorce was for some flimsy reason, it was sinful, and so was the second marriage.

As Jesus' comments in the NT clearly indicate, the wife in Deuteronomy

---

5. The word *tameh*, the general word for defilement and ceremonial uncleanness (of persons, animals, things) is used. Jeremiah uses *chaneph*, to defile, pollute.

6. Cf. I Sam. 25:44; II Sam. 3:14.

7. Otherwise, marrying a second husband (or wife) at the death of the first also would lead to defilement.

24:1-4 was "caused" to commit adultery when she married the second husband.[8]

Now we need to pull a few things together. There has been a question for some time about Jesus' comments on adultery in relationship to divorce by Christians for causes other than fornication. A vital point in that discussion that has received much attention, but that has not been adequately dealt with, is the comment in Matthew 5:32 to which I just referred: ". . . makes her commit adultery." How can that be? The answer lies in an understanding of the fact that Jesus was not speaking about marriage and divorce in the abstract. In the Sermon on the Mount He was correcting misstatements about and abuses of the OT law. The formula, "And it was said . . ." uniformly introduces a current viewpoint that represented a gross misunderstanding and/or misuse of the law. What Jesus quotes, "Whoever divorces his wife must give her a written record of the divorce," isn't a quotation from the OT at all. What it turns out to be is a misunderstanding and misapplication of Deuteronomy 24:1-4. In stressing the formality of giving a bill of divorce (a legitimate and even important thing in itself), the main thrust of Deuteronomy 24—the prohibition of easy divorce and a light view of the marriage covenant—was by-passed altogether. The focus of the passage was altered. The focus was shifted from an emphasis on the defiling and abominable nature of such a light attitude toward the Covenant of Companionship to concern about a mere formality that (though important in its place) was incidental to the major thrust of the passage.

When, therefore, Jesus speaks of *causing* the divorced wife to commit adultery, he means a wife who is divorced and remarried as the one in Deuteronomy 24 was.

Since the Pharisees persisted not only in misunderstanding divorce, Jesus makes the meaning of "defiled" even more explicit—He calls it adultery. He is saying that a wife who is divorced on "any ground" (Matt. 19:3), short of fornication, like the one in Deuteronomy 24 (who is divorced because of an *erwath dabar*—something repulsive) is caused by that divorce to commit adultery if she marries another.

The reason the husband may not marry her again even after the death of her second husband (as well as after a divorce) is that *he* has caused her to be defiled in divorcing her for a sinful reason. The defilement equals adultery. If she had been free to remarry, she would not have committed adultery when she did, and she would not be considered defiled. In Matthew 5:32 it is

---

8. Christ is thinking of a situation that fits the rubrics of Deut. 24:1-4, the passage in view in Matt. 5:31, 32.

clear that she is not really *eligible* to marry another (remember, Deut. 24 doesn't say the wife is free to marry either; it simply records the fact that, in the case proposed, she does, indeed, do so), because to do so would lead to adultery on her part as well as on the part of the second husband.

Now it is time to make a nice distinction. While it is not biblical to say that this woman is "still married to her first husband in God's eyes" (he is referred to as her "former husband"—v. 4, and she is expressly called "the wife of *another*"[9]—v. 2), nevertheless, marrying the second man constituted an act of adultery. How is that, if (as we saw earlier) divorce—even sinful divorce—really breaks a marriage?

The sinful divorce (based only on an *erwath dabar*) truly broke the first marriage; the sinful adulterous marriage to the second man was a genuine marriage (though adulterous).[10] These facts must be understood. But if they were not "still married in God's sight" why was the second marriage adulterous?

We must remember that adultery always involves a violation of the marriage covenant in such a way that a third party is introduced into the picture claiming the right (or privilege) to do for one of the two parties what they have contracted to do for one another.

Normally, adultery takes place while the marriage contract is still in effect. In the situation to which Jesus refers (Deut. 24) that contract has been broken for sinful reasons. Therefore, while it is truly broken (and no rights, privileges or obligations of marriage are permitted or required at this point), nevertheless the divorced parties *have no right in God's eyes to be in a divorced state*. They are obligated to be reconciled in remarriage so that they can renew the contract and continue to pursue their vows. That is the point (cf. I Cor. 7:10, 11). As Paul says, they must remain unmarried not only in order to be in a position to be reconciled (as we saw earlier) but, as we now see, also *in order not to commit adultery*.

Adultery, then, is sexual sin with someone other than the one with whom one *ought* to be having sexual relations. That the marriage contract has been sinfully broken means a number of things, including,

1. That the divorced persons cannot have sexual relations with one another, even though they *ought* to be doing so because they *ought* to be married. The *right* to sexual intercourse has been removed even

---

9. That is to say, no longer his.
10. As, for instance, the sinful marriage of a believer to an unbeliever is a genuine marriage.

67

though the obligation to do so in a regularized marriage situation has not.[11]

2. That anyone who marries either of the sinfully divorced persons (who are under divine obligation to remarry one another) commits adultery as well as the divorced person he/she marries, not because he/she is still married but because he/she is obligated before God to be married. He/she has no right before God to be in an unmarried state because of divorce over an *erwath dabar*.

What has just been said, Jesus assured us, applies equally to any man or woman who sinfully divorces his/her partner (cf. Matt. 19, Mark 10, Luke 16). Between the various passages in the Gospels, all the bases are covered, as the diagram that follows makes clear.

I must make a final comment on the Gospel accounts. It is vital to recognize that, unlike the Pharisees, Jesus does not restrict His discussion of divorce to Deuteronomy 24. He does not consider it the basic or definitive OT passage on the subject—it was merely a regulation that had to do with a particular kind of problem relating to marriage. Instead, He returns to the passages regarding the institution of marriage in Genesis 2. Here we see one woman for one man, united in one person (one flesh) for life. That, Jesus told them, is the way marriage is intended to be.

When Jesus asked, "What did Moses command you?" (Mark 10:4, He was thinking of the command in Genesis 2 to leave father and mother and become one flesh.[12] But the Pharisees respond by misquoting Deuteronomy 24. Then, they misapply it: "Moses permitted the writing of a certificate of divorce and the divorce" (Matt. 10:4). Their minds are focused on an entirely different point. They are not concerned about what God desired but about how far they can stretch God's law; about what is formally correct.

It is true that Moses gave the regulation, and by it acknowledged divorce—that Jesus admits (Mark 10:5; Matt. 19:8). But he did so only because of the hardness (stubbornness) of men's hearts (as we have seen, all divorce is occasioned by sin). However, Jesus goes back to the ideal: "from the beginning this was not the way it was" (Matt. 19:8). That is to say, divorce was not provided for as an option when God instituted marriage.

God treated divorce in much the same way that He dealt with polygamy

---

11. I have been speaking of sexual relations especially because of their significance in so many counseling cases at this point, but the principle applies to all the elements of companionship agreed to in contracting marriage.

12. Cf. William Hendriksen, *New Testament Commentary: The Gospel of Matthew* (Grand Rapids: Baker Book House, 1973), p. 715.

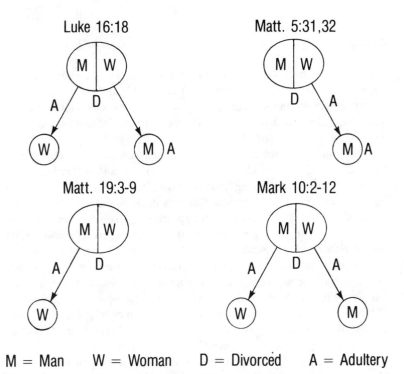

Luke 16:18

Matt. 5:31,32

Matt. 19:3-9

Mark 10:2-12

M = Man   W = Woman   D = Divorced   A = Adultery

and concubinage (cf. Judg. 8:30, 31; Exod. 21:7-9; Deut. 21:10-14). Recognition and regulation of these practices, that, like divorce, were not from the beginning, show a similar approach.

In our day cigarette smoking is not forbidden but it is heavily regulated (cigarettes can't be advertised on T.V., must carry the Surgeon General's warning, can't be smoked in certain parts of an airplane, etc.). In this one respect, the practice of smoking resembles the way divorce was viewed and regulated.

If it is true that, in the Sermon on the Mount, Jesus restored the true meaning of God's commandments (as I believe He did[1]) rather than abrogating or substituting something else for them, you will want to ask the question, "How did divorce come to be the resolution of problems growing out of the sexual sin of adultery?"

Clearly in the OT the law required stoning as a penalty for adultery (cf. Deut. 22:22; 22:23, 24; 22:13-21; Lev. 20:10). But just as clearly, we see Joseph—instead of following Deuteronomy 22:23-29—seeking to obtain a divorce. And he is not condemned for this decision but (on the contrary) commended for his kindness to Mary in proceeding to divorce her *privately*. (That seems plainly to be the point in Matt. 1:19 where, *in explanation of this contemplated action*, Joseph is called a "just" man.) Moreover, God did not put David to death for adultery, but accepted his repentance and allowed him to marry Bathsheba (who became a progenitor of Jesus Christ—cf. Matt. 1:6, in which Matthew makes a point of the fact). And, of course, in Matthew 5, 19, the Gospel passages we have been considering, Jesus also allows divorce in the case of fornication. Where did this notion of divorce-connected-with-sexual-sin originate?

Obviously, Joseph was not following some new law enacted by Jesus in Matthew 5 or 19; Jesus, Whom Mary was carrying, was the very baby in question! Did Joseph, on his own, decide to follow some later innovation of the Jewish community? If so, would God accept this purely human alteration of His law, and even make sure to commend the one who followed it? And, did Jesus' exceptional clause really *explain* the law or did it simply add to it or qualify it? To answer these questions biblically is not easy, but down that route lies an understanding of many things.

Let us begin by considering the most obvious, most basic, and (therefore)

---

1. For the argumentation on this, see standard commentaries but esp. John R. Stott, *The Christian Counter Culture* (Downer's Grove: InterVarsity Press, 1971), pp. 69-81. Notice, Jesus is referring to Pharisaic interpretation (not to Scripture): (1) He introduces the interpretation with the words ". . . it was said" (Matt. 5:31a) not with His standard formula for introducing Scripture: "it is written," (2) the quotation does not square with the passage in Deut. but with a misstatement of that Scripture passage.

easiest explanation of the origin of divorce for sexual sin. Beyond Joseph and David, we notice that in the OT God Himself recognized (and thereby taught us) that divorce for the sexual sin of adultery is an option. He taught us this by both precept and example in His own relationship with Israel. What God has taught, let no man deny!

In a number of passages, God speaks of His relationship to His OT covenant people as a marriage. As the NT makes clear (Eph. 5:22-33), this is more than a mere analogy; rather, the biblical norm for Christian marriage is found in the relationship of Christ to His church (the prototype of which was the relationship of God to His bride, Israel): as Christ . . . so too the husband; as the church . . . so too the wife.

God speaks warmly of His engagement and marriage to Israel:

"I spread My skirt over you and covered your nakedness. And I swore to you and entered into a covenant with you,"[2] declares the Lord Jehovah, "and you became Mine" (Ezek. 16:8).

This marriage relationship continued. God tenderly reminisces about Israel's first love after the betrothal in Egypt and in the early days of marriage in the wilderness (desert):

"I remember the loving kindness[3] of your youth, the love of your courtships, and your following Me in the desert" (Jer. 2:2b).

But these days of courtship and early marriage ("following") did not last. There came a change. After the marriage at Sinai and when she entered the land, Israel began to change her affections and (not once, but) continually was unfaithful to her Husband, Jehovah:

"On every high hill and under every green tree you lay down like a harlot" (Jer. 2:20b; cf. 3:23-25; 3:6, 8, 9).

And,

". . . she went after her lovers and forgot Me," says Jehovah (Hos. 2:13; cf. 2:5, 7).

And,

. . . the sons of Babylon came to her, to the bed of love; and they

---

2. N.B., as the parallelism makes evident, a marriage covenant involved vows made to one another (swearing). Yet, as we shall see, God's vows were not utterly unconditional (as some have wrongly maintained), since when Israel broke her covenant vows, He was released from His.

3. *Chesed*=covenant love; i.e., Israel's early fulfillment of her marriage vows.

71

defiled her with their fornications[4] . . . and she uncovered her fornications . . . and she multiplied her fornications (Ezek. 23:17, 18,
19).

So God said,

". . . the nudity of your fornications will be bared, even your lewdness and your fornications" (Ezek. 23:29b).

This was done as God finally divorced her:

"Israel committed adultery, I put her away and gave her a bill of
divorce" (Jer. 3:8; cf. 3:1, 2).

And,

Thus says Jehovah: "Where is the bill of divorce of your mother whom I
have put away?" (Isa. 50:1).

As a result He could say:

"She is not My wife, and I am not her Husband.[5] Let her therefore put
away her fornication from her face and her adulteries from between her
breasts"[6] (Hos. 2:2; cf. 1:9).

That God plainly and consistently connected divorce with adultery by
fornication is a fact that simply cannot be disputed. If, then, for no other
reason, we can understand why Christ, on good OT grounds, spoke as He
did in Matthew 5, 19. But, let us complete the OT story. Even then—in spite
of her sin—God loved Israel and called to her to repent and return. If she did,
He declared that He would receive her back and make her His own once
more:

"O Israel, return to Jehovah. . . . Take with you words and return to
Jehovah. . . . Say to Him, 'Take away all my iniquity and receive us
graciously' " (Hos. 14:1, 2).

Indeed, God Himself, in grace, took the initiative (as the book of Hosea
indicates) to

". . . lure her and bring her into the wilderness" [cf. Jer. 2:2b,
quoted above. The wilderness (or desert) would remind her of the early,
wonderful, pure days of courtship and marriage] "and speak to her

---

4. N.B., the word *fornications* here (and throughout) is used of a married woman. The
plural is used for the enormity of the sin, the number of ways in which Israel fornicated, the
number of times or all of the above.

5. Clearly, divorce for fornication properly broke the marriage: God and Israel were no
longer Husband and wife.

6. Fornication and adultery used in parallelism; fornication was the act that led to
adultery—the result.

heart. . . . And at that day," He declares, ". . . you shall call Me Husband" (Hos. 2:14, 16; cf. also Jer. 3:13, 14).

This wooing would win her back through repentance:

> Then shall she say, "I will go and return to my first Husband, for then it was better with me than now" (Hos. 2:7c).

When she did, God forgave and cleansed her, making her as pure as if she were still his virgin bride:[7]

> "For the Lord has called you when you were an outcast wife, grieved in spirit, and as a wife in youth who was rejected," says your God. "For a brief moment did I forsake you, but with great compassion I will gather you" (Isa. 54:6, 7).

Commenting on these verses Young and Oehler say (successively):

> Zion is set forth as a woman that in her youth had been espoused, and then because of her sins cast off, and later again called back to be the wife. . . . The phrase [wife in youth] does not refer to a woman of young age but to one whom the husband married in youth.[8]

> The adulteress has become the bride of God, as though she had never been unfaithful: "like a wife of youth."[9]

It is plain from this evidence that divorce for adultery by fornication was considered a natural option for God to use in referring to His relationship to Israel. Here we must be careful not to plead that God can do as He pleases and that His actions are not an example to us. The figure of marriage (and divorce) that He uses to explain his actions and His various relationships to Israel would explain nothing, but only confuse the reader, if, indeed, stoning alone was the way to deal with adultery. It is inconceivable that God—without some explanation—did that which was contrary to all that He requires of His own people in the same circumstance. Since in the law there is no record of God allowing for divorce on grounds of fornication, and since there seems to be no explanation for this change necessary by the time of the prophets Isaiah, Jeremiah or Hosea, we may assume that the understanding that this was allowable was already universal among God's people and had become the regular practice of the land. The very least we can say is that in these prophets, by His recognition, adoption and (implied) endorsement of the practice, God placed His approval on it.

---

7. Cf. my book *More than Redemption* for more on forgiveness: chap. 13, pp. 184-232.

8. E. J. Young, *The Book of Isaiah* (Grand Rapids: Eerdmans, 1972), III: 365.

9. Gustave Oehler, *Old Testament Theology* (Grand Rapids: Zondervan, n.d.), p. 507. See also Keil and Delitzsch.

If from no other source, Joseph and Jesus might easily have derived their view of divorce-for-fornication—just as we have here—from the example and words of God Himself.

Now, let us move one step further. It seems also that the NT Church recognized that the words of Jesus, based on God's own example in the OT, indicate that something less than stoning—namely, repentance and forgiveness—may be required for fornication-adultery in its various forms. The case in point is the sin of the unrepentant incestuous man in I Corinthians 5:9ff.[10] This idea could have been gleaned not only from God's example in relationship to Israel, but also in his treatment of David. David committed murder and adultery—both of which sins led to the death penalty. Yet when he repented (II Sam. 12:13) God said through Nathan the prophet:

> "The Lord on His part has taken away your sin; you will not die" (II Sam. 12:13).

He declined to exact the death penalty, even for this double offense.

But how could God make such exceptions to His own rules? It would seem that the case law (not the moral law) was not taken to be absolute and unbending.[11] There were some options written in (e.g., Deut. 22:29 seems absolute, but Exod. 22:16 qualifies this by giving the father [and the girl through him] discretion in the case). But it would seem also that others were understood. Jesus speaks this way when He says, "From the beginning it wasn't so," and "Moses, because of the hardness of your hearts. . . ." Here is a concession (and, in this instance, the case law itself seems to be a lessening of the creation ordinance). But Jesus does not elaborate on the basis for this concession; He simply says,

> "Moses, because of the hardness of your hearts, allowed you to divorce your wives" (Matt. 19:8).

Does He refer here to written permission in the first five books of Moses or to an unwritten, well-known practice instituted by Moses that underlay all these OT exceptions to stoning? Knowing the hardness of hearts that could lead to an indiscriminate and cruel use of capital punishment in this matter,

---

10. He was to be excommunicated not for his sin of incestuous fornication but for his arrogant refusal to repent (cf. I Cor. 5:2). When he confessed and forsook his sin, he was forgiven, comforted and reassimilated into the church (II Cor. 2:1-11). Lev. 20:11; 18:8 called for stoning for this sin. Evidently, the man's father was still living, since his step-mother is called a *wife*, not a widow. This would be a form of adultery.

11. Is there a distinction between the emphatic expression "he shall *surely* be put to death" (Num. 35:17, 18, 21; cf. Berkeley for an even clearer translation) and the simple statements found in Deut. 22:22? Does the former indicate a more absolute form than the latter?

did Moses agree to divorce for fornication-adultery as an alternative that Christ reaffirmed (v. 9)? If so, the exception would be of long-standing as Israel's history seems to show that it was.[12]

It would be hard to establish a case either way, and I shall not speculate further. What is certain—whenever the practice originated (whether under Moses or later on)—the practice of divorce for adultery was sanctioned by God in the OT period. Christ did not introduce some new law in this regard, and Joseph evidently was well within the scope of God's directive will in the matter.

---

12. This is not totally speculation. If, as I have shown, Christ's reference to Deut. 24 (in Matt. 5:31, 32) and the proper understanding of "defiled" in Deut. 24:4 means that the case in question concerned a divorce sinfully given because it was for a ground other than adultery, there is good reason to suppose that Moses had given such a ruling, which, in the Gospel accounts, Jesus was reaffirming.

PART III   REMARRIAGE

CHAPTER 13

Remarriage

We have seen something of the biblical picture of marriage and divorce. It remains for us to discover what the Scriptures tell us about the remarriage of divorced persons.

To begin with, we must look at remarriage in general; then, we shall consider whether God allows divorced persons to marry. Finally, we must ask, "If divorced persons may remarry, who among them may, and under what conditions?"

Remarriage

What of remarriage? Does the Bible allow, discourage, encourage or tolerate remarriage? In the Bible, there is nothing, *per se,* against remarriage after the death of one's spouse. The Bible states,

> But if her husband dies, she [the surviving spouse] is free from the law, and if she marries a different man she isn't an adulteress (Rom. 7:3b).

That statement is clear: it is not wrong to remarry.

Indeed, in some instances, remarriage is *encouraged.* For example, in I Timothy 5:14, Paul wrote:

> I want younger widows to marry, to have children, to run their own homes, and give the opponent no opportunity for insult.[1]

Paul could see the possibility of temptation, scandal, busybodiness and the placing of unnecessary burdens on the church to support widows, unless they remarried. So, for practical reasons, and for the testimony of God's Name, he gave this direction to the church through Timothy. Far from finding anything wrong, or even problematic, about remarriage itself, then, here we see it strongly advised.

Moreover, Paul went so far as to *command* widows who are having

---

1. The Book of Ruth is a good example of how favorably the Scriptures look upon remarriage. It is interesting how a whole book deals with the question, and that in the line of Christ there are remarried persons.

difficulty restraining sexual desire to seek remarriage as a means of dealing with that problem (and, note, this requirement occurs in a passage generally discouraging marriage because of an impending crisis):

> To the single men and to the widows I say that it is well for them to remain like me. But if they can't control themselves they must marry, since it is better to marry than to burn (I Cor. 7:8, 9).

Finally, consider Paul's words in I Corinthians 7:39:

> A wife is bound to her husband for so long as he lives. But if her husband dies she is free to marry anyone that she wants to, but only in the Lord.

Plainly, the concept of remarriage not only was entertained by the New Testament church, but very favorably entertained. Of that there can be no reasonable doubt.

Polygamy

In the light of that fact it would seem strange for Paul to forbid the church to appoint someone as an elder or deacon who is a remarried man. Yet that is exactly what some teach. This error arises from an incorrect interpretation that has been placed on the words "the husband of only one wife," which occur in I Timothy 3:2, 12; Titus 1:6.

Of course, opponents to remarriage are thinking about divorced persons remarrying when they arrive at this interpretation. But their view proves too much: not only does it exclude divorced remarried persons from the two offices in the church but all remarried widowers as well!

That is strange, I say, not only because it excludes from office some of the most highly qualified persons in many congregations, but it conflicts with the fact that—as we have seen—the NT always speaks favorably about remarriage and, indeed, in some situations even commands and encourages it. It would be a great surprise to discover such an interdict. If for no other reason, that conflict should make us wary of the interpretation of the phrase "the husband of one wife" that makes it mean one only and never (even after the death of one's spouse) another.

Is there another interpretation?

Yes, there is, and there is every reason to prefer it to the former. There was a perfectly good Greek word that Paul might have used (*gameo*) to indicate that one could *never* remarry (even after the death of his spouse) and hold office in the church if that is what he had wanted to say. Then the phrase would have read: "married (*gameo*) only once." That would have been

80

clear. But he did not use *gameo*; indeed, he was not talking about how often one was *married*. Rather, Paul consistently used the unusual construction "the husband of only one wife." He was concerned *not* about how many times a man had been married, but about how many wives he had!

The phrase "the husband of only one wife," strictly speaking, permits only one interpretation: a prospective elder or deacon (because he must be an example in all things—including his marriage practices) may not be a polygamist. The phrase means "the husband of only one wife" *at any given time*. It says nothing whatsoever about remarriage.

The OT permitted polygamy, but it was never the ideal. (In Genesis God said the *two* shall be one flesh—not the *three* or *five* or *eight!*) But in the NT, while a polygamous convert was allowed to enter the body without putting away his wives (on the principle stated and reiterated in I Cor. 7:17, 20, 24), he could not become an officer. The life of an officer must be exemplary and God wanted the example of monogamous marriage held before the church.

But we are told by advocates of the anti-remarriage viewpoints that there was no polygamy in NT times. The facts prove otherwise; they are wrong. Polygamy not only continued among the Jews, but also among the Greeks and Romans (and who knows where else?).

Many of the early converts of every church that Paul began were Jews of the dispersion. Josephus twice mentions polygamy in his day. In A.D. 212, the *lex Antoniana de civitate* made monogamy the law for Romans, *but specifically excepted Jews!* Later, in A.D. 285, Diocletian found it necessary to rescind the exception, but in 393 Theodosius found it necessary to enact a special law against polygamy among the Jews since they persisted in the practice. Even that did not put an end to it; polygamy among the Jews continued until the eleventh century.[2]

But that isn't all. Greek marriage contracts indicate the existence of polygamy in New Testament times. One such contract, from 92 B.C., reads,

> It shall not be lawful for Philiscus to bring in another wife besides Appolonia.[3]

This marriage contract makes it clear that, apart from such a prohibition, polygamy was an altogether likely option. The law enacted in A.D. 212, mentioned above, also indicates the presence of polygamy in the Roman

---

2. Eugene Hillman, *Polygamy Reconsidered* (Maryknoll: Orbis Books, 1975), pp. 20, 21.
3. Hunt and Edgar, *Select Papyri*, op. cit., I: 5-7.

world. That the clause against polygamy in the marriage contract just cited was not a rare exception is shown by a similar one in another contract from 13 B.C.:

Ptolemaeus . . . shall not . . . insult her nor bring in another wife.[4]

"Well, then, if Paul did not forbid remarriage among elders and deacons," you ask, "What of divorced persons holding office?" In response, let me close this chapter by quoting an article, previously published in *Matters of Concern for Christian Counselors*,[5] that deals with this important question:

Question: "A man has been nominated as an office bearer in a church. He, his wife and those who nominated him are very upset over the fact that his nomination has been refused. The refusal was due to a church by-law that states that no divorced person may ever hold office in the congregation. They say, "God has forgiven; why doesn't His church forgive?" What is the scriptural position on this matter?

Because this problem is an urgent one in so many situations, I have responded to this question in a general manner.

Answer: Your question is not unique. In this day of many divorces and remarriages the church is facing such issues more and more. The matters you raise are important. They cannot (and should not) be avoided. On the other hand, they are not easy.

First of all, let's make two things clear:

(1) God does forgive *all* sins in Christ. The couple are absolutely correct about this. There is only *one* unforgivable sin, the sin against the Holy Spirit (attributing the Holy Spirit's work to an *unclean* spirit—the devil). I Corinthians 6:9-11 makes it clear that Christ grants forgiveness for the sin of adultery.

(2) Forgiveness does not clear one from every consequence of his sin. Forgiveness means that God will not hold one's sin against him. The forgiven person will not be judged eternally for that sin; Christ was judged in his place. But social consequences must still be met. If, in a drunken brawl, an unsaved man shoves his arm through a plate glass window with the result that the arm must be amputated, that does not mean that later, when he is saved, he sprouts a new one. No, he will bear the consequences of that sin for life.

Now, there are consequences of sin that are for life, and some that are not. The only issue in question is, how does the Bible speak about this particular question?

The answer, it seems, is that the Bible teaches that some consequences

---

4. Ibid., p. 11.
5. Cf. *Matters of Concern for Christian Counselors*, pp. 75, 76.

of past sin for eligibility as an officer in Christ's church are lifelong, and others are not. For instance, if before conversion a man married more than one wife, his polygamy does not keep him from membership in Christ's church, but it does prohibit him from bearing office in that church.[6] And this is not because he isn't forgiven by God and the church, but because an office bearer must "be an example in all things" (including monogamous marriage practices).

Now is the question at issue like that? Not quite. A qualification for an office bearer is that he "must be above reproach" (I Tim. 3:2) and also "must have a good reputation with outsiders" (I Tim. 3:7). Titus reiterates this by saying he "must be blameless" (Titus 1:6).

The circumstances of his divorce and/or remarriage may be such that a person for years afterward (perhaps even for the remainder of his life) would fail to qualify because of the bad reputation that he bears as a result. On the other hand, his lifestyle subsequently may be such that God has changed his reputation. Moreover, he may not have sinned at all in obtaining a divorce, if it was granted on biblical grounds.

Since each case differs, and since we have these clear biblical criteria to determine who is eligible for office, it is wrong to add church by-laws, especially when they are less flexible than the Scriptures themselves. The church has no right to forbid what God allows. It is the job of the existing officers in each instance to determine whether or not a given individual fits those qualifications.

On the other hand, if the man in view also is "very upset," and if this means anger, lack of self-control, etc., or if his conversion is quite recent, other qualifications would apply (cf. I Tim. 3:2, 6; Titus 1: 7, 8). The attitude with which they deal with this matter itself will say much about qualifications, and (from another perspective) may have a lot to say about the reputation of the nominated office bearer.

---

6. He must be "the husband of one wife" (i.e., only one at a time—I Tim. 3:2; Titus 1:6). The passages do *not* say "married only once" (the normal word for marriage, *gameo*, is not used in these passages).

CHAPTER 14

Remarriage after Divorce

In the previous chapter we saw that remarriage, in itself, was well thought of in the NT church. But now we must consider the problem of remarriage *after divorce*. This issue is complex, and (again) an emotionally charged one. Let us patiently pursue the ground in a calm and orderly fashion.

We are frequently told, in one way or another, that the story changes. The favorable attitude toward remarriage is exchanged for condemnation. "After all," we are assured, "the only NT word on the subject is in Matthew 5, 19 and the parallel passages, and that word is a warning against adultery. The NT says nothing of remarriage for divorced persons in a positive way." But that simply is not true. In I Corinthians 7:27, 28a we read:

> Are you bound to a wife? Don't seek to be released. Have you been released from a wife? Don't seek a wife. But if you do marry, there is no sin in doing so.

There are several particulars regarding this passage that should be noted:

1. The word translated "released" in both instances is the same word, *luo.*
2. To be *released* from a wife in the second instance must mean what it does in the first or the intended contrast that is set up would be lost.
3. It is plain that divorce is in view in both instances. Clearly, when Paul says that one must not *seek* to be released from a wife he doesn't mean by death! The release in view can mean only one thing—release by divorce. So too, the release in the second instance must refer to release from the bonds of marriage by divorce (N.B., to be "released" is the opposite of being "bound" to a wife).
4. Paul allows for the remarriage of those released from marriage bonds (i.e., divorced) even in a time of severe persecution when marriage, in general, is discouraged (v. 28).
5. And, to boot, he affirms that there is no sin in remarrying.[1]

It is most important, then, to understand that the position of those who hold that under no circumstances whatever may a divorced person remarry,

---

1. That Paul is not speaking of a virgin marrying in 28a may be seen from the fact that in 28b he speaks of that subject. Obviously 28a is a continuation of the subject introduced in v. 27. Paul is speaking to the previously married who have been divorced.

is totally unwarranted. This passage is fatal to that view; the Scriptures plainly contradict it when they affirm the opposite. There can be no doubt about it, the Bible allows the remarriage of some divorced persons (not those in view in Matt. 5, 19, etc.).

The question must be put more sharply. To call "sin" what God expressly says is not sin (v. 28)—wittingly or unwittingly—is a serious error that cannot be ignored or lightly passed over (cf. I Tim. 4:3). In effect, it amounts to placing the traditions of men (whose motives may be good, but whose judgment seems clouded) above the Word of the Lord by adding restrictions and burdens that God has not required us to bear. This can (and does) lead to nothing less than confusion, unrest and division in Christ's church.

There is further evidence that remarriage to divorced persons was not unknown or prohibited. In Ezekiel 44:22 we read.

> Nor shall he [a priest] marry a widow or a woman who has been divorced; only a virgin of the house of Israel or the widow of a priest.

I do not wish to discuss the ceremonial reasons for this prohibition, but simply wish to point out that the rule singled out the priest as *special*. There were other such rules that pertained to priests alone that made them *special*. Clearly by practice (from Abraham onward—cf. Gen. 23:1; 25:1) and by precept (as we have already observed) the Bible not only *allows* but often *encourages* the remarriage of widows. Yet, here, the priest is forbidden this right (unless the widow was the wife of a priest). It is not that the remarriage of widows is wrong, but that priests are in a special class *and may not do what it is perfectly right for others to do*. The same may be said of the second prohibition in the verse, "or a woman who has been divorced." Priests may not do *what others may:* i.e., marry a divorced person. The whole force of the verse is to specify requirements peculiar to priests. If no one was allowed to marry a divorced person anyway, the prohibition would be pointless. Only if the practice was generally acceptable is the verse of significance, since only then would it mark out an exception to the general rule. [2]

Nothing in the Bible forbids the remarriage of divorced persons without obligations, except to priests, who were exceptions to this policy. It is assumed in the Bible that wherever Scripture allows divorce, remarriage also is allowed. [3]

So, thus far, we have established two *very* significant points:

---

2. Cf. also Lev. 21:7, 13-15.
3. Remember too, that the right of remarriage was expressly stated in both Greek and Hebrew divorce certificates. The *Talmud* says, "The essence of the *git* [divorce document] is the words 'Behold, you are hereby permitted to any man.' " *Gittin 85b*, op. cit., p. 439.

1. Remarriage, in general, is not only allowed but in some cases encouraged and commanded. It is looked upon favorably in the NT.

2. Remarriage after divorce is not disallowed, but in cases where one has been properly "released" from his spouse it is plainly declared to be no sin—even in perilous times of crisis when all marriage is discouraged. There is no reason to believe that the New Testament's favorable view of remarriage does not apply equally to all such cases.

Let us now turn to a third matter. Who may remarry after divorce and under what conditions? The answer to those questions is at once both simple and complex. What is simple is the first general principle:

All persons properly divorced[4] may be remarried.

That is what I Corinthians 7:27, 28a teaches, and the principle fully accords with I Corinthians 7:15 in which one who is divorced according to the biblical provisions stated there is free and no longer bound. If he is free, he is free to remarry.

What is complex is whether persons who were divorced improperly (because the divorce itself was sinful), and as a result, who are still under an obligation to be reconciled to their spouses, or whether persons properly divorced but with other obligations (to be discussed later) can so discharge these obligations that eventually they too may be free to marry.[5]

John Murray has argued successfully that a person who has been divorced in accordance with the exception stated in Matthew 19:9 is free to remarry because the exception ("except because of sexual sin") applies not only to the phrase "whoever divorces his wife," but also to the phrase "and marries another."[6]

I shall not (could not) redo here the fine exegetical work that he has done to support this conclusion. I commend to you his discussion. Assuming, therefore, that Murray is correct, it is altogether proper to say that in such cases—there being no obligation for the parties to be reconciled—one could remarry without committing adultery.[7]

---

4. By *properly divorced* I mean those who are released without obligations. N.B., I Cor. 7:27 speaks of those who are *bound* to a wife being released from *those very bonds*.

5. The principle that runs throughout the Scriptures, in one form or another, is that God has called us to peace (I Cor. 7:15). God requires us to set all unsettled matters to rest; He wants no loose ends dangling (cf. the *Manual*, pp. 52-62).

6. Cf. Murray, *Divorce*, pp. 36-43.

7. It is interesting to note that the Scriptures record no threat of stoning for remarriage while one's spouse is alive. Yet if it were always adultery to do so, one would expect to discover at least a hint of it. Only here in Christ's words in Matt. 19:9 is the fact that adultery can result from remarriage under conditions of obligations raised. This observation is pertinent to what I have discussed in chap. 12 about the origins of divorce for adultery. Christ's words about divorce in

It is proper, then, for *some* divorced persons to remarry just as after the death of a spouse (cf. I Cor. 7:39) so long as they "marry in the Lord" (i.e., Christians must marry Christians. When they are free to marry, they are not free to marry any and every person; they may marry only believers). But, applied to the remarriage of divorced persons, that biblical ruling can have some very interesting (and vexing) implications. To begin with, it is clear (for instance) that if a Christian man divorces an unsaved wife *who wants to continue the marriage,* he has sinned (cf. I Cor. 7:12, 13). Upon repentance, he must seek not only God's forgiveness for this sin (and all other sins committed in the course of obtaining the divorce), but *her* forgiveness as well. Because he *ought* to be married to her (he divorced her *against* the clear biblical prohibitions in I Cor. 7:12-14) he must seek to return to her and reestablish the marriage. However, he is no longer married to her, and because he is required to marry "only in the Lord," he is blocked by that rule from doing so and thus fulfilling his obligation. His sinful disobedience has led him into a bind. What does he do?

1. He informs her of his dilemma. She, seeing his repentant allegiance to the Lord may be led to consider Christianity anew. But beware of a false profession on her part, if she deeply wants her former husband to return.
2. Continue to pray for her salvation.
3. Evangelize her.
4. Refrain from dating or marrying another.
5. Unless his former wife (now or at a later point) makes it clear that she no longer desires to become reconciled and remarried to him, he must wait and pursue her conversion and their subsequent remarriage.
6. If she does come to the point of no longer wishing to remarry him, he is free (I Cor. 7:15).

It is obvious that he has placed himself in a dilemma from which repentance and forgiveness alone will not extricate him. At this point, prayerfully, he must throw himself on God's mercy.

This case illustrates some (but not all) of the difficulties that often accompany divorce. We may wonder why matters should become so complex. The basic answer is clear: sin complicates life. And when, in addition,

---

the Gospels, as we have seen, refer (in part) to Deut. 24:1-4. The wife, in that discussion, would be "defiled" because her husband (if he did what the husband in Deut. 24 did) would cause her to commit adultery by divorcing her for a cause lesser than sexual sin (they would be obligated to be reconciled because they *ought* to be married rather than unmarried). Yet, neither the woman nor the second man who married her was stoned for the act (after all, she was still alive after the first and second divorce!). Presumably, at least in such cases, we could say that Moses didn't require stoning for adultery.

there is a sinful response to the initial complications of sin, the tangle can become quite intricate at times. Counselors—and congregations—have no choice in the matter; they must unthread the mess until they have dealt fully with every strand.[8]

Sometimes complications also arise from the sin of the church in failing to do what God requires; this always comes back to haunt the church in days to come. Many of the difficulties that result could have been avoided if the church had done what it ought to do at the outset.

Let us take, for example, what could have been a relatively simple situation, but which was muddied by the church's poor advice and inaction. (Usually it is the hands-off stance of the church that accounts for the problems. But difficulties rarely ever "go away" if we do nothing). In this case, Mary and Joe are professed Christians. Neither has committed adultery. Joe divorces Mary because he is "tired of arguing and fighting about everything." The ground of the divorce is incompatibility (a non-biblical ground). The church got involved only *after* the divorce occurred. Joe, in unrepentant anger,[9] left the church and when the pastor called to see why, he read him the riot act, said that he didn't care to remain in a church where people said such things, and demanded that his letter be transferred to a congregation up the street. The first church, in fact, did send a letter of his good standing to the second church (the pastor and church officers actually breathed a sigh of relief when they did so). But now the chickens finally have come home to roost: Mary has met another Christian man and wants to marry him. (Joe has not remarried.) The first church has what they call a "strong stand" against remarrying divorced persons under circumstances where the former spouse is alive and unmarried;[10] what should the pastor do?

Well, because of his own failures, and the failures of the officers of the church, the pastor and officers have brought this complication on themselves. Originally, the church should have entered the picture early—at the *very* latest, when Joe went to see the lawyer (good shepherding usually picks up problems of this magnitude much sooner). On the basis of I Corinthians 6 (and other passages) Joe should have been required to disengage the lawyer since to file for a divorce is sin. Among other points, he should have been instructed that

8. For more on how to sort things out see *Matters of Concern*, pp. 20-23.

9. A member (not the pastor or an officer) told him that he had sinned in divorcing Mary.

10. This is typical of many churches in which this "strong stand" actually grows from great weaknesses in the care and discipline of members. The place to be "strong" is where the *Bible* is; not where it isn't!

1. God has forbidden him to take his wife—a professed believer in Jesus Christ—to court. All such problems as he and Mary have must be resolved by the church within its jurisdiction and not before pagans at court.

2. God has required him to take the Matthew 18:15ff. route in order to resolve these problems.

3. God has not allowed for divorce on the grounds of incompatibility.

4. There is no reason why the marriage cannot be *transformed* if both parties desire it for God's glory.

If Joe had agreed to these admonitions, then there would have been no divorce, reconciliation could have been effected and counseling toward a new sort of lifestyle could have begun. It would have been work; but the situation would have remained fairly simple.

If Joe had failed to respond positively, this sin would have complicated matters a bit more, but if Mary (and the church) had pursued the Matthew 18:15ff. procedure faithfully then—assuming (as does Matt. 18:15ff.) that Joe stubbornly refused to cease and desist from his sinful plans to divorce Mary on unbiblical grounds—at length (after all attempts had been made to bring about reconciliation) Joe would have been excommunicated and the whole matter would fall under I Corinthians 7:15. Mary's position, and that of the church would be clear—she would be free to marry another. The outcome, once more, would be clear and uncomplicated.

However, because the church (*both* congregations were wrong in different ways) failed to advise and act as they ought (a typical scene in evangelical churches today), many new complications have arisen making it harder for everyone concerned. Here are some of these complications:

1. Mary isn't free to remarry.

2. Joe has been deprived of his rights to church discipline.

3. Joe hasn't been confronted at all levels according to the requirements of Matthew 18:15ff. and is still considered a member of Christ's church in good standing despite his rejection of Christ's authority in the Bible.

4. A sinful divorce has been ignored.

5. Joe (and Mary) stand in peril of committing adultery.

Now, can anything be done to rectify the situation? Yes, but it will be complex, messy and harder on all concerned. Avoiding the original mess—as it always does—has brought on a far worse one (Spurgeon once said "It is easier to crush the egg than it is to kill the serpent"). How does one bring order out of chaos? Here is (among other things that may arise along the way) basically what must be done to bring about a peaceful settlement of all the issues:

89

1. The first church must seek God's forgiveness, forgiveness from Mary and Joe, and from the second church for failing to handle matters scripturally. This step cannot be omitted without destroying everything.
2. Next, Mary must be advised to go seek reconciliation with Joe faithfully following the procedures of Matthew 18:15ff. step by step.
3. Joe should be called upon to repent and seek reconciliation with Mary and his former church (and the member against whom he expressed such anger).
4. If all goes well, Mary and Joe will be reconciled, remarry and build, under proper care in counseling, a new and better marriage (not go back to the same old things[11]).
5. But, let us suppose Joe sinfully refuses to be reconciled. Accordingly, his sin further complicates. But that should not stop the process.
6. In that case, Mary should pursue Matthew 18:15ff.
7. But this time she must ask Joe's new church to become involved (at least in the final stage of the Matt. 18:15ff. procedure) since he is now under their discipline.
8. By this time, of course, they would be aware of what was happening since Mary's congregation (sometime before) should have contacted them, seeking forgiveness and alerting them to the new action that Mary has been advised to take, and the possibility of involving them in discipline should Joe not respond to the early steps of the procedure.
9. If Joe's church does what it should, well and good. Joe will repent or will be excommunicated, setting the matter to rest.
10. But what if Joe's church fails to assume its responsibilities and will not excommunicate Joe even though he fails to heed advice? This sin on the part of the church further complicates matters. Nevertheless, we still have recourse.
11. Then, the officers of Mary's church must humbly confront the officers of Joe's church (it might begin with pastor confronting pastor; but if that fails, officers confronting officers) to try to resolve the matter, offering help, support, direction, encouragement, etc.
12. If Joe's church agrees, well and good. All will flow naturally to one of the two presented ends: reconciliation or discipline. But what if Joe's church refuses? Obviously, as it has all along, their sin further complicates matters.
13. Mary's church, at that point, has only one alternative left—only to be used with great caution when *every* effort has failed—to declare (by a functional judgment) Joe's church to be as no church since it refuses to hear Christ's authority, and Joe (as a part of the organization) to be *as* a heathen and a publican.
14. At long last, all threads have been pulled; the matter is set to rest, and on the basis of I Corinthians 7:15 Mary is eligible to marry another.

I have gone through this elaborate process, not to discourage church

---

11. Cf. *More than Redemption*, pp. 174-183.

discipline, but (rather) to encourage its use at an early point for the benefit of all. Only then, can many of the complications be avoided. Nevertheless, since churches have been failing to discipline (and presumably many will continue to), you will need to know what to do (as Mary, as a pastor, as a church officer) in order to clean up the many messes that you may encounter along the way. The basic principles, with variations to meet each case, can be used in any number of situations.

The question of the past record of converts and of repentent Christians often arises in discussions of divorce and remarriage. We must not avoid it.

Converts have all sorts of sinful irregularities in the past. They have become "involved in every sort of uncleanness," as Paul puts it in Ephesians 4:19c. How should this past be viewed when considering remarriage? Should we haul out the record, review it in detail, and on the basis of what we find determine one's eligibility for marriage? Yes and no. Let me consider the no. Some want to rehash every detail, irrespective of its relevance to the issue of remarriage. That's plainly wrong, as most would agree. Others even go so far as to advise breaking up present marriages on the basis of unbiblical divorces in the past.[1] Others want to forbid the remarriage of all divorced persons. And still others, also looking at the past, want to prohibit all those that they call the "guilty parties" from remarrying. What does the Bible say? May divorced persons with past guilt remarry?

There are, of course, any number of complications that might arise. Because it is impossible to mention all of the possible combinations, I shall deal only with general principles. These principles must cover such diverse situations as the following examples pose: Suppose unsaved relatives marry within the forbidden degrees of consanguinity and now become Christians. Should they dissolve their marriage? A prostitute is converted. Now she has met a Christian man who wants to marry her (fully aware of her past).[2] A man who has divorced two wives for incompatibility. He has now become a Christian. Must he go back to one of his unsaved wives?[3] If so, which? Or may he marry a believer—a third wife, forgetting his past?

To these, and scores of other possible situations, the Bible has an answer. When a person is converted, he is to

> . . . remain with God in the state in which he was when he was called. (I Cor. 7:24; cf. vv. 17, 20, 26).

---

1. Cf. the controversy among the churches of Christ reflected in Jas. D. Bales' book, *Not Under Bondage* (Arkansas: Bales, Searcy, 1979).

2. Prostitutes do not consort with unmarried persons only, but continually commit adultery. Is such an adulteress eligible for marriage?

3. See the previous chapter for more on this problem.

Paul made this a rule for all the churches (v. 17). This implies that a convert, from the date of his conversion, starts a new history from square one.[4] The same emphasis is apparent throughout the Scriptures (e.g., cf. I Cor. 6:9-11). Adulterers, fornicators, and homosexuals, as well as others with notorious records, are said to be "cleansed, washed, sanctified." We read in I Corinthians 6:11, "Such *were* some of you" (N.B., the past tense: Paul no longer considered them such after Christ's cleansing by the Spirit.) It seems well-established that once a believer was forgiven and had forsaken a sin, he was no longer considered a fornicator, a drunkard, etc. Why then should we continue to call a breaker of the covenant of companionship such?

It is clear that God forgives murder, sexual immorality of the basest sort, etc. *The church must do so too!* And it is important to note that forgiveness (even in the case of a repentant *believer* who sinned after conversion), involves not only cleansing but comfort and restoration to full fellowship among the members of Christ's church (II Cor. 2:7, 8).

Somehow or other, adultery and divorce-for-unbiblical reasons seem to be omitted from today's accepted list of forgivable sins, even though God forgave them. That is a tragic mistake. To omit such sins is to defile the human heritage of Jesus Christ Himself!

By that, I mean to say that, in the line of Christ, one finds that Rahab the harlot (an adulterer) married Salmon and entered the line of the Messiah. David and Bathsheba also plainly committed adultery (not to speak of David's murder) and Jesus is called the "son of David." Was the union of David and Bathsheba from which Christ came adulterous? Or was it sanctified by forgiveness?

We must not be more pious than Paul (or God Himself!). Who among us has not sinned? What reader of these pages is not an adulterer and murderer in his heart? Who is to cast the first stone? Are you better than Rahab, David or Bathsheba in God's sight because you have not outwardly committed adultery as they did or because you have not entered into marriage with an unbiblically-divorced person and by that committed an act of adultery?

Why have adultery and divorce been singled out from among the list of heinous sins recorded in the NT?[5]

I am not trying to minimize the sinfulness of divorce on unbiblical

---

4. That doesn't exclude the necessary fulfillment of civil or moral obligations. True repentance always leads to such fruit.

5. N.B., sinful divorce doesn't even appear among the items on these lists found principally in Matt. 15; Rom. 1; Gal. 5; II Tim 3; Rev. 21, 22, yet greed, slander and lying are there!

grounds. It is heinous and its consequences are tragic.[6] But if we are to view it in some special light, as so many present-day Christians do, how is it that the NT doesn't do so? Would it not have appeared at or near the head of every such list of abominations, if the NT viewed sinful divorce as we do?

We must say, therefore, that what God has cleansed no man must call unclean. Christ is bigger than our sin—even our sin of adultery and divorce. We minimize Christ when we speak and act as if this were not so. These sins are truly heinous; we must not minimize that fact either. But Christ is greater than sin—*all* sin. We don't minimize sin or its effects, then; rather, we always maximize Christ and the power of His cross.

Sometimes the case of Herod is cited (Mark 6:17-18) to try to demonstrate that remarriage is sin. But the facts do not support the case. When John the Baptist challenged him, and sought to bring him to repentance by citing his violation of God's law ("it isn't lawful"), it is important to distinguish between several things:

1. This is not a case of remembering what has been forgiven; John's goal was to bring Herod to repentance leading to forgiveness. Herod was an unrepentant man who had never sought God's forgiveness.
2. John's words did not declare Herod's marriage to a divorced woman sinful; that was not the point. He said, "It isn't right for you *to have your brother's wife*" (Mark 6:18b). This is the point—Herodias had been married to Herod's brother. To marry her (on any basis) would violate Leviticus 18:6, 16.[7]

Let us ask the question, then, Is marriage to formerly adulterous or sinfully-divorced persons prohibited? Ask another: Is marriage to former murderers or liars or slanderers prohibited? There is no more biblical reason to believe that the first is prohibited than there is to believe that the second is. Either God's cleansing cleanses or it does not.

That is why we are so often incorrect in speaking of the "guilty party" and the "innocent party" in considering remarriage. This language isn't biblical and must be used only with great care. While at the time of the divorce one party may have been *guilty* (of sinfully obtaining a divorce) and the other *innocent* of it, it is not proper to *continue* to speak of the *repentant, forgiven* person (whether his sin was committed before or after conversion) as the "guilty" party. In Christ, he is now innocent. Who are we to remember and hold that guilt against him when God does not?

---

6. Consequences also may follow the forgiveness of a sin (cf. *More than Redemption*, pp. 230ff.). But the NT fails to indicate any necessary consequences *that the church must impose* on sinfully-divorced persons after repentance.

7. Cf. Josephus, *Antiquities*, 18:5:1; 5:4.

Let's talk about this so-called "guilty party" a bit. Loraine Boettner is absolutely right when he says,

There is no law in the Bible which says that he must remain unmarried.[8]

Clearly, God allowed the marriage of David and Bathsheba to stand even though both of them had been guilty of adultery, and David of murder as well. No more sordid beginning to a marriage could be imagined. Yet, God blessed that marriage in time because forgiveness was granted, the past was cleansed, and the future was cleared for God's blessing (cf. II Sam. 12:13; Psa. 51; esp. v. 2). If this marriage, which *at its inception* was knee-deep in sin (David didn't repent until *after* the marriage) could be blessed by God to the bringing forth of the Messiah, why do we say that persons who are forgiven and cleansed before marrying, cannot expect God to bless their marriage because of sin in their past?

Now, someone will say that this makes forgiveness too easy and will encourage divorce. I do not honor that argument any more than Paul did in Romans. Divorce, wrongly obtained, is *sin*—a heinous offence against God and man. I am not encouraging divorce any more than God encouraged robbery, adultery, homosexuality, lying and murder by declaring that such sins are totally forgiven in Christ and put into the past (I Cor. 6:11). Repentance, when genuine, is like David's repentance (Ps. 51, 38, etc.); it is not treated lightly as a gimmick. A repentant sinner recognizes the serious nature of his offense and is not only grateful but produces fruit (change) appropriate to repentance. In any discussion of divorce and remarriage we must be careful to preserve the integrity of two biblical truths.

1. Sin is heinous.
2. Grace is greater than the most heinous sin (Rom. 5:20).

So, we have seen that (1) remarriage after divorce is allowed in the Bible and that the guilty party—after forgiveness[9]—is free to remarry.

There is one other issue to be mentioned. When I asked (at the beginning of this chapter), "Should we haul out the record [of the past], review it in detail, and on the basis of what we find determine one's eligibility for marriage?" I answered equivocally, "Yes and no." It is time to examine the yes. There are some matters from the past that may yet be present even after

---

8. Loraine Boettner, *Divorce*, (Phillipsburg: Presbyterian and Reformed Publishing Co., 1960), p. 32.

9. The church should always ascertain that the party has sought forgiveness, should grant it and should determine (and note in the elders' minutes book) that it has been granted. When all obligations have been fulfilled and the party is free to remarry, this too should be noted.

forgiveness. They must be set to rest and put (where they too belong) into the past. Before declaring a repentant, wrongly-divorced person free to remarry another, we must ask:

    1. Have you freed yourself of all past obligations?

    2. Have you sought forgiveness not only from God but from your former wife, children, relatives, others involved?

    3. Have you made every effort at reconciliation[10] (where possible)?

    4. Have you made every effort to right all wrongs (so far as possible) regarding such matters as

        a. voluntary repayment of any unfairly-obtained monies, rights, etc., in a divorce settlement,

        b. assuming obligations for child-support, etc.

Moreover, since a past divorce proves that there has been a failure in marriage we must

    1. counsel all formerly-divorced persons before remarriage about any sins in their lives that may have contributed in some way to the outcome,

    2. counsel them about any wrong attitudes or ideas about marriage (or marriage partners) that he may have developed during the previous marriage and the divorce proceedings with a special emphasis on love as giving, not getting.

I assume that good marriage counseling will be given to him as to every other person who gets married.[11]

Note

Some have suggested that the wedding of a divorced person not take place in the church building. That is plainly wrong. First, it views the church building as something that it is not—a sanctuary (i.e., an especially holy place). But of more importance, if a marriage is right, it is right *all the way*—and the church of Jesus Christ should say so. Nothing should be done to indicate in the slightest way that forgiveness is not complete. Jesus Christ saves! In the minds of some a church wedding symbolizes a proper marriage, and a white gown, a holy wedding—then, *by all means*, be sure to conduct all such weddings in the church building and let the white wedding gown symbolize the cleansing of the blood of Jesus Christ. Let there be no spot or wrinkle, or any such thing! Let us proclaim to all who will hear the overwhelming grace and amazing forgiveness of Jesus Christ in *every legitimate* way!

---

    10. Cf. chapter 14 for a special case, and the procedures to follow.

    11. See the program on premarital counseling in my *Shepherding God's Flock* and in Howard Eyrich's *Three to Get Ready* (Phillipsburg: Presbyterian and Reformed Publishing Co., 1978).

CHAPTER 16

Dealing with Divorce and Remarriage

If there is one thing that has become clear throughout this study it is this—cases of divorce and remarriage are complex; they are not as simple to deal with as some seem to think. I am not referring to the heartaches, the broken lives, the struggles, the shattered expectations and much more like that. To consider such matters—and they *ought* to be considered—would involve at least two or three more books. But, I refer simply to the complexity of the principles and procedures that must be applied. The sin (and, in particular, the failure to handle it and its consequences biblically) itself is complex enough.

Is there a way of summarizing what has been said? Can we develop a check-list that (together with the content of the entire book) may be used to analyze and determine particular cases? The following list of principles and questions, although admittedly incomplete, will help you to do so. Be sure to consider each in every case where it is applicable.

I. *Principles:*
   A. Marriage:
      1. is a divinely-ordained institution,
      2. is the first and most fundamental institution,
      3. is covenantal and binding,
      4. is a covenant of companionship,
      5. is the place for true intimacy,
      6. is to conform to the model of Christ and His church.
   B. Divorce:
      1. always stems from sin,
      2. is not necessarily sinful,
      3. always breaks a marriage,
      4. is never necessary among believers,
      5. is legitimate on the grounds of sexual sin,
      6. is legitimate when an unbeliever wishes to divorce a believer,
      7. is forgivable when sinful.
   C. Remarriage:
      1. in general, is desirable,

2. is possible for a divorced person,
3. is possible for a sinfully-divorced person through forgiveness,
4. is possible only when all biblical obligations have been met,
5. is possible only when parties are prepared for marriage.

II. *Questions:*

1. Are all, one or none of the parties Christians?
2. Who wants the divorce?
3. On what grounds?
4. Does this party *really* want a divorce, or only a change in the situation?
5. Has I Corinthians 6 been violated?
6. Has sexual sin been present?
7. Is there acceptable evidence for such sin or only hearsay and/or supposition?
8. Has church discipline (Matt. 18:15ff.) been applied?
9. If so, what was the outcome?
10. Is there repentance/forgiveness?
11. Is reconciliation required?
12. Does an unbeliever want the marriage to continue?
13. Has a former spouse remarried another?
14. Did any church fail to handle a divorce/remarriage properly?
15. If so, how? And what must be done to set this straight?
16. Is the believer in a state where the church may declare him/her free from all obligations and, therefore, free to remarry?
17. If not, what more needs to be done to bring about this condition?

Conclusion

I considered the possibility of running all sorts of cases past the principles and procedures that I have set forth in this book to demonstrate better how they can best be applied. But I decided against doing so (perhaps at a later point I can do this in some other context):

First, one could never think of all of the possible situations encountered.

Second, I wanted to make this book available to the Christian community at large—laymen and pastors, counselors and Bible students. To consider all sorts of cases would have made it much larger and more expensive. Both of these factors would have tended to reduce the readership.

Third, I have many other things to do, and to include these cases would have delayed the publication of this book by several months, at least. Since there is a great demand for its publication, I determined to release it right away.

My prayer is that God will use this book to bring balance and blessing to His church. I have written with those two purposes in mind.